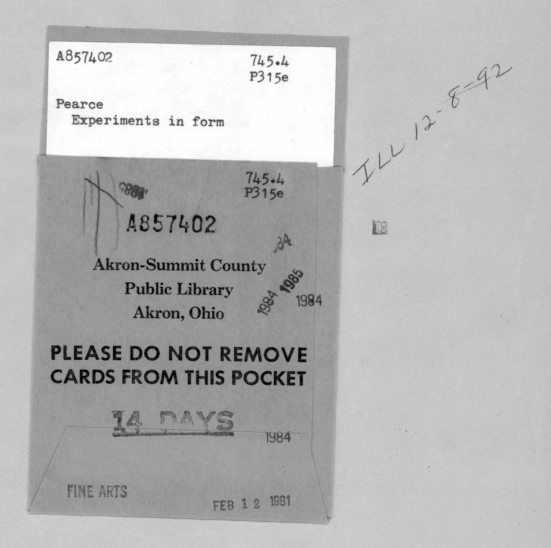

Experiments in Form

A Foundation Course in Three-Dimensional Design

Peter Pearce
Susan Pearce

 VAN NOSTRAND REINHOLD COMPANY
New York Cincinnati Toronto London Melbourne

To the memory of two great teachers,
Charles Eames and D'Arcy Wentworth Thompson

Copyright © 1980 by Peter Pearce and Susan Pearce
Library of Congress Catalog Card Number 80-10353
ISBN 0-442-26497-6

Printed in the United States of America.
Illustrations and book design by Susan Pearce and Peter Pearce.

Published by Van Nostrand Reinhold Company
A division of Litton Educational Publishing, Inc.
135 West 50th Street, New York, NY 10020, U.S.A.

Van Nostrand Reinhold Limited
1410 Birchmount Road
Scarborough, Ontario M1P 2E7, Canada

Van Nostrand Reinhold Australia Pty. Ltd.
17 Queen Street
Mitcham, Victoria 3132, Australia

Van Nostrand Reinhold Company Limited
Molly Millars Lane
Wokingham, Berkshire, England

16 15 14 13 12 11 10 9 8 7 6 5 4 3 2 1

Library of Congress Cataloging in Publication Data

Pearce, Peter.
  Experiments in form.

  Bibliography: p.
  Includes index.
  1. Design. I. Pearce, Susan, joint author.
II. Title.
NK1510.P34   745.4   80-10353
ISBN 0-442-26497-6

Contents

Preface

The material for this book draws upon my experience as a teacher of basic design. Although I have not taught in any formalized program for eight years, teaching is a subject that is dear to my heart and one to which I continue to give considerable thought. Since my days of teaching, I have been primarily occupied with issues related to the design, manufacture, and marketing of product systems in my own company, Synestructics, Inc. My interest in fundamental philosophical and theoretical questions, however, is as strong as ever.

My book, *Structure in Nature is a Strategy for Design* (MIT Press, 1978), deals extensively with the fundamental principles of modular structure. I have always considered that work an extended study of basic design principles, and I've also always believed that the extent to which effective design is possible is governed, in large part, by one's understanding of fundamental principles. The great designers in history have been those with a strong sense of fundamentals in some form or other.

The basic principles of design do not stem from what is fashionable but are rooted in pure phenomena. Design curricula that do not include a good basic design program risk depriving their students of preparatory experiences that will help them avoid the tyranny of temporal fixations. Although the historical antecedents of this book are to some extent rooted in the Bauhaus—I myself graduated from the Institute of Design in 1958—we hope that we have moved in a different and new direction, one more responsive to the complexities and opportunities of the world as we have come to know it.

The material in Part I comes, in its entirety, from my earliest experience as a teacher of basic design. The remarkable examples of solutions to the various design problems in Part I were all done by freshman students of mine at California State University at Northridge from 1961 to 1965. Teaching those students was an exciting experience for me, and I wish to thank them all for sharing it with me. I have used some of the same problems with students in other institutions, and other teachers who followed me have used some of these problems. To this day, I have never seen any better or more varied solutions to these basic design problems than the examples shown in Part I.

The evolution of the material in Part II also began at Cal State Northridge in the early '60s. In its simplest original form, Part II is a problem that has subsequently been used by other teachers. The level of comprehensiveness and complexity to which it has evolved, however, is presented for the first time in this book. There was an evolutionary stage to the problem which briefly appeared when I was a faculty member in the School of Design at the California Institute of the Arts, and its evolution has been a continuing interest of mine ever since. As time passes, it seems to me to be of increasing relevance. Indeed, my fascination with this problem sequence is probably the main reason we decided to do this book. If the reader finds one-tenth the fascination I did with the subject matter of Part II, then I believe the book will have justified itself. The examples of problem solutions in Part II were all created especially for this book by the authors with the dedicated and deeply appreciated help of Diane Gould.

Part III draws, to some extent, from my earlier book mentioned above but also includes much new material. Chapter 6 of Part III pays homage to all of my favorite designers and many of my favorite design products, structures, and projects. The selections are unashamedly biased. I hope the inclusion of some of my own work will not be viewed as a gesture of immodesty by virtue of its association with such illustrious company, but that its presence is justified by its instructional usefulness.

I have felt for many years that if the designer is going to rise to the opportunities available for making a contribution to the world, philosophical attitudes must be developed and refined beyond the superficial. We have attempted to move in that direction with this book, and we hope that in some modest way we can help young designers to consider their intentions with utmost care. We also hope that the adventurer who actually takes on the challenge contained in the following pages will be able to share in the pleasure we enjoyed in developing and attempting to solve the problems ourselves.

We gratefully acknowledge funding for this book, which was provided by a grant from the National Endowment for the Arts, Washington, D.C.

Peter Pearce
November 1979
Studio City

Introduction

As a foundation course in three-dimensional design, the purpose of this book is to provide experiences of first principles, which are applicable to those professions concerned with the design of the built environment regardless of its scale or scope. By design, we mean the deliberate act of creating or giving form as a solution to a problem for which a physical result is required. The intent of these experiences is to provide a basis for understanding how a variety of factors, influences, phenomena, constraints, and intentions govern the decisions which give rise to physical design form.

The term, three-dimensional design, includes the fields of architecture, planning, industrial design, interior design, and related activities. It may also include sculpture. From the standpoint of the attitudes represented by this book, a more appropriate subtitle might have been, "a foundation course in physical design." The classic approach to basic design courses, and as a consequence, to design attitudes in general, has been the aesthetics of appearance as the dominating influence. Although this approach has its important aspects, it has led to a three-dimensional built environment dominated by arbitrary form.

The didactic purpose of this book, then, is to foster an understanding of formative processes that will lead the designer of the built environment toward solutions which are consistent with first principles in nature, i.e., those which are energetically conservative, adaptive, and functional. The creation of arbitrary form—that is, form created without regard to its "fit" with natural phenomena—is often a source of inefficient and ineffective use of material, energy, and human resources.

To minimize the arbitrariness of form in the built environment is to maximize its performance. To maximize performance is to accomplish objectives in the most effective manner while minimizing the use of energy and material resources. This is not necessarily to say that design objectives should be compromised in order to save natural resources, but it does suggest that design objectives should be performance oriented. One of the limitations of a "visual effects" approach to form is that it encourages a direction that is not particularly sensitive to performance-oriented solutions.

The fulfillment of performance requirements is at the root of all natural structure. If an organism does not fulfill its function or if it does not perform efficiently, it does not succeed. Fitness is determined by effectiveness, and effectiveness is a function of efficient least energy performance. In nature, forms and structures are created according to principles of least energy, i.e., natural first principles. This fact is explored in great depth throughout what must be one of the great books on design in nature—*On Growth and Form* by D'Arcy Wentworth Thompson (Cambridge University Press, 1963). In his book, Thompson describes the formative processes in nature as least energy responses to the actions of forces: "In short, the form of an object is a diagram of forces that are acting or have acted upon it; in this strict and particular sense, it is a diagram."

In an effort to direct formative processes in design along lines which minimize arbitrariness and maximize performance orientation, the notion of form as a diagram of forces emerges as an important governing principle. If you say, "Oh yes, I see what you mean—form follows function," beware. Although that infamous slogan certainly had its usefulness in its time, the notion of form as a diagram of forces is one of far greater subtlety and depth. In the realization of any physical object that becomes part of the built environment, it must emerge into reality first from some kind of design strategy. A design strategy that incorporates the notion of form as a diagram of forces may offer the real possibility of generating forms that are responsive to the human needs and natural requirements of diversity, adaptation, change, and the conservative use of natural resources.

In order to facilitate a design strategy based upon the principle of form as a diagram of forces, we offer an elaboration on the concept of force. In the simplest and most general sense, a force may be considered any governing influence that may act to determine the form of a particular design solution. In nature, the form of any structure is determined by the interaction of two fundamental classes of forces: (1) intrinsic forces and (2) extrinsic forces.

Intrinsic forces are those governing factors which are inherent in any particular system; that is, the internal properties of a system which govern its possible arrangements and its potential performance. Extrinsic forces are those governing influences which are external to any particular system. They are the inventory of factors, largely environmental, which give direction to the form options allowed by the inherent form-giving properties (intrinsic forces) of a given physical system.

All forms in nature are determined by the interaction of intrinsic and extrinsic forces. For example, the possible external shape options that a given crystal such as a snowflake may take [5.1] are controlled by the internal symmetry of the atomic arrangement—that is, by the system with which the atoms themselves are arranged. The particular form of a given snow crystal is the result of the least energy interaction of external environmental factors (e.g., temperature, humidity, wind velocity) with the inherent principles governing the atomic arrangements. A given crystalline substance may take a variety of shapes, but certain limitations of form, usually expressed as angular relationships, are governed by the inherent form-giving properties—the intrinsic force system—of the atomic arrangement. Consequently, although there is an infinite number of different shaped snowflakes, they all exhibit the symmetry of a six-sided regular hexagon.

Examples of the interaction of intrinsic and extrinsic forces to produce form in nature are relatively simple and comprehensible with respect to inanimate crystals as they tend to be dominated by physical-geometric phenomena. The process is much more complex and elusive as one examines biological form and structure. The delineation between intrinsic and extrinsic forces is not always clear and tends to be hierarchical. That is, at one scale a force may be considered extrinsic, but in a larger context, the same force may become intrinsic. This hierarchical phenomenon exists for both inanimate and animate structures. Each successive level of structure is the environment (extrinsic force system) for the preceding level (intrinsic force system).

In the creation of the man-made environment, extrinsic forces can be considered the design goals—the various whimsical, philosophical, aesthetic, or performance-oriented criteria which may be imposed on the design form. Intrinsic forces in the design of the man-made environment can be considered the "state of the art" technologies and the limitations of their use governed by the level of skill and perceptions available and by the dogma of habit and bias that may prevail.

If we assume, then, that designed form is the result of the interaction of extrinsic and intrinsic forces, the quality of the results will be determined directly by how well those forces are understood. For extrinsic forces, the design objectives and their physical embodiments must be carefully identified. For intrinsic forces, the limitations within which practical and efficient physical solutions are possible must be found. *Experiments in Form* attempts to provide an experiential base for understanding such a formative process and the extent to which it leads to high performance-effective solutions— solutions consistent with the high performance, energetically conservative, adaptive, and functional first principles in nature.

This book is intended to be a guide for self-instruction, although it may readily be used by faculty as a program guide for basic design classes. A series of directed exercises or problems are given which are designed to provide a direct empirical background with a variety of design principles of gradually increasing complexity. The problems are designed, not only to provide a background of relevant experience, but so that the criteria for successful solutions are unambiguous.

In such an approach, the student as empirical explorer can evaluate his own work as it progresses, while understanding a basis of form and structure in which arbitrary decisions are minimized. The implications of cause and effect for design realization become apparent by the nature of the problem and the criteria which must be fulfilled by its solution. For the alert student, an "expert" is not needed to tell him how well or poorly he has solved a particular design problem. Degree of success will be apparent from the unambiguous criteria (extrinsic forces) and the inherent limits of technique (intrinsic forces).

At some point, however, feedback is helpful and stimulating, and hopefully even gratifying. With this in mind, an exemplary solution is provided for each problem. Materials that are relatively easy to work with, such as paper, cardboard, wood, and plastic foam, are used to solve the problems. Skills, techniques, tools, and equipment required for a solution are described and cross-referenced. Only those materials and methods that do not involve sophisticated equipment will be required.

The book consists of three conceptual parts. The three parts are thematically related, but each has its own appropriate organizational scheme consistent with the material being presented. Part I consists of a sequence of theoretical problems requiring the synthesis of intrinsic and extrinsic forces in a self-contained solution. These problems will require the design and construction of three-dimensional structures which embody efficient responses to given force categories in the physical world. The problems in Part I, which use humble materials, call for the invention of solutions derived from data which has been collected primarily through direct empirical means. This sequence is considered a warm-up for the parts that are to follow. It deals primarily with problems associated with the fundamentals of structure and materials properties and includes an introduction to ergonomic considerations.

In Part I, Chapter 1 consists of six problems all organized in the same format. The statement of the problem is given, followed by a summary of the extrinsic and intrinsic forces. Quantified performance standards are given, where appropriate, as an aid to evaluation since all six problems must be responsive to performance criteria. Applicable techniques and materials are presented followed by a discussion of conceptual guidelines. In this first chapter, no solutions are given or even hinted at. This is done deliberately so that the student who is sufficiently disciplined and so inclined may proceed to solve each problem before checking the answer. In so doing, an important sense of discovery can be experienced.

Once a solution has been accomplished, upon turning to Chapter 2, a collection of exemplary solutions to all six problems is presented. The solutions represent varying degrees of success, and a surprisingly diverse range of excellent solutions is exhibited. It becomes apparent that there is an extensive array of possible solutions to almost any problems.

Students who choose to examine the exemplary solutions prior to proceeding to their own solutions, will no doubt be stimulated by what they see. This may lead to solutions at higher levels, or it may lead to frustrations in the difficulty of the challenge. The sense of discovery may be limited. Whatever one's style may be, whether solving the problems prior to seeing the answers or after, both are valid learning experiences. The main objective of the problems is to develop one's own solution through direct physical experimentation to the point of having a testable structure that will perform. It is in this direct experience that the highest levels of understanding are reached, and as such, this book is intended not as a reading exercise, but as a program of direct experience.

Having completed the warm-up from Part I, it is time to get down to business. Part I is a preparation for Part II, and Part II, consisting of Chapters 3 and 4, incorporates the essential concerns of this book in a comprehensive sequence of integrated problems. Part II consists of nine problems in which a complete three-dimensional design experience is provided. Numerous aspects of intrinsic-extrinsic force interactions are investigated as an interrelated whole. The same phenomena, which are the concern of the individual problems of Part I, are in this second part integrated into a complete design solution.

The organizational format of Part II differs from Part I in some important respects. The statement of the problem is given along with a summary of extrinsic and intrinsic forces. Quantified performance standards, however, are not given since they are neither readily available nor necessary for the evaluation of problem solutions. This is true in spite of the fact that, once again, such solutions must be responsive to performance criteria. In Part I, quantified performance criteria

are possible and useful because such objectives are extremely simple. In Part II, performance objectives are complex, and although amenable to analytic evaluation, they do not lend themselves to quantitative interpretation. Indeed, solutions which are responsive to performance criteria in this second part must be governed by a sense of appropriateness. This sense of appropriateness is not a call to be arbitrary, but it represents the degree to which arbitrary gestures are minimized.

In Part II, conceptual guidelines are discussed along with descriptions of techniques and materials. The techniques become more sophisticated and much more involved. Concepts and skills learned, however, in Part I are directly applicable to the problems in Part II. An important difference between the first two parts is that in Part II, an exemplary problem solution is given along side the problem statement. It is in the nature of this integrated problem sequence that no learning value is to be gained by withholding exemplary solutions. Indeed, because each successive problem is derived directly from the preceding problem, it is a necessary condition of understanding that solutions be illustrated along the way. In addition, the complexity of this problem sequence is such that there is an infinite number of solutions within the constraints of the extrinsic and intrinsic forces. Also, unlike the problems of Part I, elementary discovery is not particularly important in this second part.

At the end of Part II is a two-page spread which shows in a sequence of views a summary of the many aspects of this integrated problem. Once again, it is the doing, the working out in the realities of three-dimensional physical space that is important here. Reading this book may be helpful, but if it has real value to the student, it will be as a guide through an introductory design experience.

Part III, Chapters 5 and 6, deals with real world examples that illustrate the design principles we have been exploring. Here we are particularly concerned with the principle of form as a diagram of forces and its various corollaries of performance, efficiency, adaptation, and function. Examples of form in nature are presented in Chapter 5, and examples of form in the built environment are shown in Chapter 6. Part III could probably be the first part as well, and we encourage its use alongside the working-out of the problems of the first two parts. Part III is intended to serve as a frame of reference and perhaps a source of inspiration. It can also be a source of correlation between the theoretical problems and the realities of form in the world. It may provide further insight into the rationale behind the investigations of Part I and the integrated problems of Part II.

In the third part, it is our intention to provide some good examples that are consistent with the attitudes presented in this book. In the case of the examples in nature, which demonstrate the principle of form as a diagram of forces, the selection is infinite. We have chosen examples that are relatively graphic and which may be understood, for the most part, rather directly without the need for extensive technical knowledge. We hope that a good intuitive sense of the least energy behavior of formative processes in nature can be gleaned from the limited number of examples presented. Patterns of form and structure in nature are quite clearly the principles upon which design sensibilities and strategies must be based.

In the realm of built form, examples which are truly representative of the principle of form as a diagram of forces are difficult to find. The examples selected are few and represent our personal biases. The fundamental consideration in determining whether a built form can be considered a diagram of forces is the extent to which performance criteria dominate the design process. Even when looking thoroughly at the built environment, it is difficult to find very many objects which suggest by their appearance that fulfillment of performance objectives was a primary design strategy. This is true of most of the architecture we see and certainly of most consumer products, the most conspicuously arbitrary of which is the American automobile.

There are certain consistent exceptions to arbitrary form in the environment. The most obvious of these is the airplane in which the superfluous is a clear impediment to performance. From a posture of immutable necessity, the form of an airplane must be absolutely dominated by performance objectives. The form of bridges and other engineering structures also tend to be dominated by performance objectives. Again, this is a matter of necessity. Accomplishments of built form, where the failure to perform would have dire consequences, always tend to be of less arbitrary design. Product areas where performance objectives become highly focused or even exaggerated can be instructive from the posture of form as a diagram of forces. Such built forms as high-performance racing cars, hang gliders, specialized instruments, and manufacturing equipment can be useful sources for clues toward understanding how built form can be a diagram of forces.

We encourage you to consider the discussion in Part III as you fearlessly pursue the problems of Parts I and II. We do not promise that what lies ahead is going to be easy or that everyone will agree with the premises. Indeed, we hope that it is quite demanding and challenging. We are not embarrassed to suggest that an active commitment to this book should be made. We believe the effort will be rewarded with pleasure of new knowledge and experience, and that this modest book can be a guide through a special set of experiences that can prepare future designers for the choices and responsibilities that lie ahead. We hope that our foundation course will be helpful, stimulating, and relevant. In short, we hope that it performs.

Part I
Some Investigations of Structure
and Form: A Warm-Up

Chapter 1:
Problems

Problem 1: Paper Tower

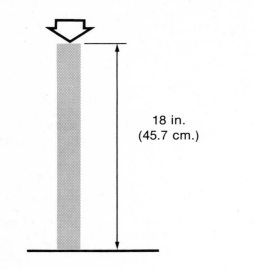

Problem: Alternative A
Design and construct a paper tower that is 18 inches (45.7 cm) high and that supports as much weight as possible. The tower is to be made from a 12 inch by 18 inch (30.5 cm × 45.7 cm) piece of construction paper such as the type commonly used in school.

Extrinsic Forces
Ultimate possible load and dimensional specifications of 18 inches (45.7 cm).

Intrinsic Forces
Configuration of tower, properties and size of material, quality of construction, nature of joining substances (glue), and techniques of their use.

Performance Standards
A weight of 20 to 25 pounds (9 to 14 kg) can be supported by this paper tower.

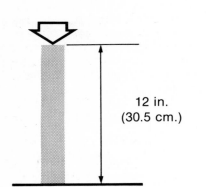

Problem: Alternative B
Design and construct a paper tower that is 12 inches (30.5 cm) high and that can support 8 pounds (3.6 kg) of weight. The tower is to be made from bond paper and is to be of the least possible weight.

Extrinsic Forces
Given load, height of tower, and requirement of minimum weight.

Intrinsic Forces
Configuration of tower, properties of bond paper, quality of construction, nature of joining substances (glue), and techniques of their use.

Performance Standards
Better performing structures have been in the weight range of .5 to .6 ounces (14–16 g).

Techniques and Materials

Folding and cutting is permissible. Cement or glue (white glue is recommended) may be used only for joining purposes, not for the reinforcement or stiffening of surfaces. Two-faced tape may also be used for joining where appropriate. Measure, cut, and glue carefully, and use glue sparingly.

After the structure has been laid out and measured, cut carefully with scissors or an X-Acto knife with a #11 blade (or similar knife). Poor craftsmanship and carelessness can have an extremely adverse effect on the performance of an otherwise well-conceived structure.

Any folding should be done with extreme care to avoid any unwanted kinks or wrinkles — sure ways to build failure points into the structure. Folds should be laid out and scored with pointed, but dull, instruments such as ball-point pens.

Conceptual Guidelines

The most cursory observation will tell you that paper is an inherently flexible material and has no apparent ability to support weight. A flat piece of paper is relatively useless in supporting the weights specified in this problem. Careful experimentation, however, will quickly reveal a fundamental structural principle: if something flat is made three-dimensional by some form of design reorganization, its strength is dramatically increased. The simplest way to illustrate this principle is to introduce a curvature, which is the same as a fold, into the material. The increased strength is immediately obvious.

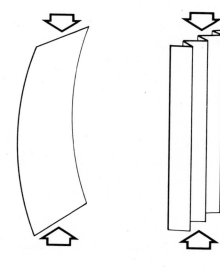

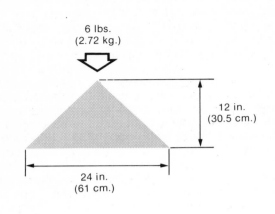

6 lbs.
(2.72 kg.)

12 in.
(30.5 cm.)

24 in.
(61 cm.)

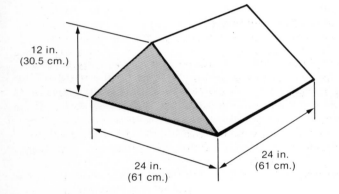

12 in.
(30.5 cm.)

24 in.
(61 cm.)

24 in.
(61 cm.)

Problem 2: Paper Bridge

Problem
Design and construct a bridge structure that can support 6 pounds (2.72 kg) of weight at its center. The structure is to be made from paper and is to be of the least possible weight. It must clear 12 vertical inches (30.5 cm) at its center and must span 24 inches (61 cm). The 6-pound weight may be any size (a brick works well), and may be supported by the structure at any height above 12 inches, as long as it is centered on the structure. A triangular-shaped object of the dimensions indicated in the figure must be able to pass under the structure without interference. The span may not be fastened down or tied across the base plane. The bridge must support its load when it is standing on a relatively smooth surface such as Formica.

Extrinsic Forces
Applied load, dimensional specifications, and minimum weight requirement.

Intrinsic Forces
Geometry of configuration, properties of materials, and quality of construction.

Performance Standards
Better performing structures have been in the weight range of 1.25 to 1.5 ounces (36–42 g).

Techniques and Materials
Paper heavier than bond, such as school construction paper, is recommended. Paper that is too heavy is not satisfactory since it will not only result in a weight penalty, but will simplify the task of supporting 6 pounds (2.72 kg), thereby minimizing the learning experience.

Glue or cement may be used (white glue is recommended) only for joining purposes, not for reinforcement or stiffening of surfaces. Two-faced tape may also be used. Measure, cut, and glue carefully, and use glue sparingly. After the structure has been laid out and measured, cut carefully with scissors or an X-Acto knife. Poor craftsmanship can

Compression Member (Column)

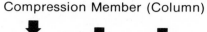

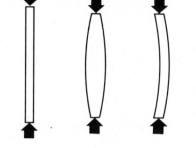

Tension Member

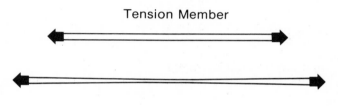

Beam

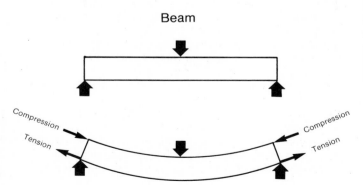

have an extremely adverse effect on the performance of the structure. Folds should be laid out and scored with a pointed, but dull, instrument such as a ballpoint pen.

Conceptual Guidelines

The tower of Problem 1 can be considered a *column.* The kind of load or force acting on a column is that of *compression.* Columns are simple structures—easy to understand and analyze. When compression members (columns) fail, they expand barrel-like as they tend to shorten, or more likely, they buckle. The strength of a compression member for a given material is governed by the ratio of its diameter to its length. A short thick column will support more than a long thin column.

The bridge is a more complex problem than the tower. It can incorporate combinations of columns, as well as members loaded in *tension* such as cables; or, as is often the case, it can incorporate members involving both tension and compression loadings such as beams.

When tension members begin to fail, they tend to stretch and become thinner around the middle. The strength of a tension member for a given material is governed by its thickness regardless of its length. A long tension member will have approximately the same strength as a short tension member of the same thickness (cross-sectional area).

When beams begin to fail, they bend. When loaded, the top side of a beam tends to shorten as in a compression member, and the bottom side tends to lengthen as in a tension member.

An efficient (high strength to weight) bridge design will reflect the interplay of the elements of structure—tension and compression—in an optimum combination. A structure in which these elements have been conscientiously considered will take best advantage of the inherent properties of the materials used in its construction.

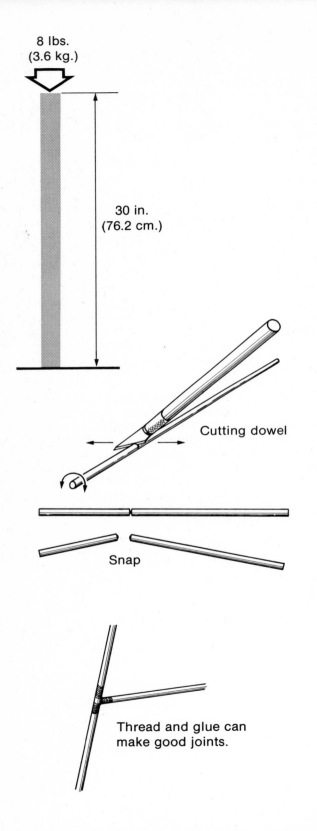

8 lbs.
(3.6 kg.)

30 in.
(76.2 cm.)

Cutting dowel

Snap

Thread and glue can
make good joints.

Problem 3:   Stick Tower

Problem
Design and construct a tower that can support
8 pounds (3.6 kg). The tower must be 30 inches (76.2
cm) high and must be of the least possible weight.
It is to be made from ⅛-inch (.318 cm) diameter
hardwood dowels, button thread, and glue.

Extrinsic Forces
Applied load, dimensional specifications, and
minimum weight requirement.

Intrinsic Forces
Configuration of tower, properties of materials,
relative scale of materials, e.g., diameter of dowel
compared to height of tower, and techniques and
quality of construction.

Performance Standards
Better performing structures have been in the
weight range of .7 to .9 ounces (21–27 g).

Techniques and Materials
Hardwood dowels, usually birch, typically come in
lengths longer than will be necessary to build the
tower. Appropriate lengths will have to be cut.
Dowels are easily cut with an X-Acto knife by rolling
the dowel back and forth with the sharp edge of the
blade. Once the dowel has been cut about halfway
through, it may be easily snapped apart.

Precut dowel components may be joined together
with thread and white glue, contact cement, or
model airplane cement. When used with patience,
white glue is significantly stronger than the others.
Glued joints can be neatly lashed with thread to
increase their strength and to ease construction.
The thread can also be used as tension members in
the structure.

As always, quality of craftsmanship is extremely
important to the performance of a well-designed
structure. Measure, cut, and assemble with great
care. Alignment of the completed structure is
extremely important if it is to perform efficiently.

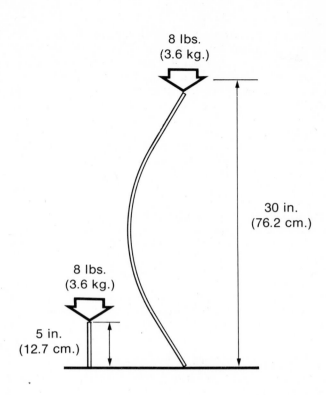

8 lbs.
(3.6 kg.)

8 lbs.
(3.6 kg.)

5 in.
(12.7 cm.)

30 in.
(76.2 cm.)

Conceptual Guidelines

Like the paper tower of Problem 1, this problem is essentially one of creating a column. Unlike the paper tower, however, it is a column of some degree of complexity. The paper column is essentially a monolithic, homogeneous structure with a constant cross-section, while the stick tower will be a multi-component, articulated structure.

There are some basic characteristics of the ⅛-inch dowels to be observed. If two different lengths are cut, say 30 inches and 5 inches, we will find that, even though they are of the same material and same cross-section, the shorter length offers sub-stantially more resistance to applied compression loads. An 8-pound load can easily be supported by the 5-inch dowel (assuming it will not fall over). The same load will readily buckle the 30-inch dowel. This is a verification of the principle discussed in Problem 2—for a given material the strength of a compression member is governed by the ratio of its diameter to its length. This suggests that longer compression members can be formed by some kind of bracing or by the use of a succession of short members.

An efficient tower design will reflect the careful consideration of the behavior of compression members as well as a possible useful role for tension members. Button thread will be surprisingly strong when loaded in tension; but if it is used (as in bracing, for example), it must be understood that it cannot be expected to resist compressive forces as well. It can easily be seen that typical tension members are completely ineffective in their resistance to compression loads.

Problem 4: Stick Bridge

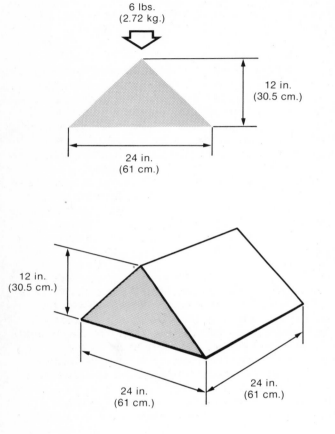

6 lbs.
(2.72 kg.)

12 in.
(30.5 cm.)

24 in.
(61 cm.)

12 in.
(30.5 cm.)

24 in.
(61 cm.)

24 in.
(61 cm.)

Problem
Design and construct a bridge structure that can support 6 pounds (2.72 kg) of weight at its center. The structure is to be made from ⅛-inch-diameter hard wood dowels, button thread, and glue and is to be of the least possible weight. It must clear 12 vertical inches (30.5 cm) at its center and must span 24 inches (61 cm). The 6-pound weight can be any size (a brick works well) and can be supported by the structure at any height above 12 inches so long as it is centered on the structure. A triangular-shaped object of the dimensions indicated in the figure must be able to pass under the structure without interference. The span may not be fastened down or tied across the base plane. The bridge must support its load when it is standing on a relatively smooth surface such as Formica.

Extrinsic Forces
Applied load, dimensional specifications, and minimum weight requirement.

Intrinsic Forces
Geometry of configuration, properties and relative scale of materials, and techniques and quality of construction.

Performance Standards
Better performing structures have been in the weight range of .6 to .7 ounces (16–20 g).

Techniques and Materials
Standard length dowels will have to be cut into different lengths as required. Use the same techniques for cutting and joint-making as described in Problem 3, stick tower.

Once again, quality of craftsmanship is extremely important to the performance of a well-designed structure. This point cannot be overemphasized. Measure, cut, and assemble with great care. It is most important on this bridge structure that, under load, the forces are distributed symmetrically from the central loading point. A careless measurement or sloppy joint can prevent this optimum distribution of stress.

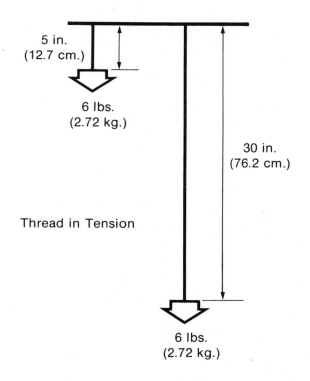

5 in.
(12.7 cm.)

6 lbs.
(2.72 kg.)

30 in.
(76.2 cm.)

Thread in Tension

6 lbs.
(2.72 kg.)

Conceptual Guidelines

Like the paper bridge and stick tower, the stick bridge is a structure of considerable complexity. If anything, it is potentially even more complex than the preceding two structures. It may offer, however, the greatest opportunity for innovation, and perhaps more than any of the other problems so far, can manifest the concept of "form as a diagram of forces."

Like the stick tower, the stick bridge will be a multi-component, articulated structure. However, just as we have struggled to overcome what could be described as the elastic quality of wood dowels (in appropriate lengths) in the design of the stick tower, we may be able to use these same properties in surprisingly advantageous ways for the bridge.

In the tower we began to see how the proper use of tension members resulted in the saving of weight. With the wood dowels we were able to demonstrate the simple concept that the strength of a compression member is proportional to its length compared to its diameter.

In like manner, using button thread, we can verify an equally simple concept about tension members. Cut a 5-inch (12.7 cm) and a 30-inch (76.2 cm) length of thread and hang weights from each of them. We can quickly demonstrate that the strength of a tension member is governed by its cross-sectional area independent of its length. Indeed, both lengths of thread will hold the same weight.

In the process of such experimentation, what becomes even more remarkable is the load capacity of the thread. Typical button thread can hold the entire 6 pounds with ease. Since tension members can function so well, perhaps we should consider their use as a weight-saving strategy.

On the other hand, it can be very tricky to take advantage of tension members. An interesting observation can be made about the comparison of compression members and tension members. Although tension members have remarkable load capacities with respect to what often seems such a small amount of material (cross-section), they typically have no ability to resist compressive forces at all. However, compression members, in most materials other than stone and masonry, can often function very well in the resistance of tension forces.

These principles of tension and compression will have to be considered carefully in the design of a stick bridge. It will be important to understand which members will have to resist only compressive forces, only tensive forces, or a combination of the two where the forces are in a state of equilibrium with the possibility that the stress will go either way. In the development of a solution to this problem, remember that the goal is to transmit the centrally applied load to the ground in the most direct and efficient manner as in a "diagram of force."

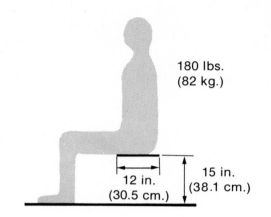

180 lbs.
(82 kg.)

12 in.
(30.5 cm.)

15 in.
(38.1 cm.)

Problem 5:   Cardboard Stool

Problem
Design and construct a cardboard structure of the least possible weight that is of sufficient strength to hold a sitting person who weighs 180 pounds (82 kg). The sitting platform (seat) must have a minimum average width or diameter of 12 inches (30.5 cm) and must be 15 inches (38.1 cm) from the ground.

Extrinsic Forces
Applied load, dimensional specifications, minimum weight requirement, and nature of applied load.

Intrinsic Forces
Configuration of structure, properties and relative scale of materials, and techniques and quality of construction.

Performance Standards
Better performing structures have been in the weight range of 18 to 24 ounces (510–680 g).

Techniques and Materials
Ordinary chipboard should be used. Do not use corrugated cardboard. Cutting, folding, and gluing is permissible. Contact cement or white glue is recommended. Two-faced tape may also be used where appropriate. Measure, cut, and glue carefully. As you have already learned, poor craftsmanship and carelessness can have an adverse effect on the performance of the structure.

Lay out and measure precisely and carefully cut out components with an X-Acto or mat knife against a straight-edge. Folding should be done by scoring against a straight-edge with a stylus. Avoid kinks and tears when folding.

Conceptual Guidelines

Before proceeding with the construction of a full-scale chipboard structure, it is advisable to do some developmental work using smaller scale paper models. Later a full-scale "rough" test structure will be useful before proceeding to the fabrication of the final design. The basic principles of your design can be quite thoroughly worked out, tested, and evaluated with paper scale models. Half-scale, or even quarter-scale, is convenient depending on what you need to discover about a given configuration and its complexity.

Cardboard is a very strong material when used properly. Pay careful attention to its inherent properties—how it facilitates some possibilities but precludes others. Think of the cardboard as an intrinsic force system. Consider the connections carefully as they can make the difference between an efficient and inefficient structure. Finally, don't forget that someone has to sit "on" the structure—a force to be reckoned with.

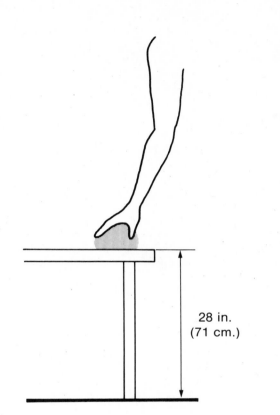

Problem 6: Table Leaner

Problem

Design and fabricate a rigid form that can comfortably support the human hand while leaning on a table 28 inches (71 cm) high. The form should be comfortable for any size hand and should be stable on the table surface. It should be as compact as possible, and extraneous material should be eliminated. Its surface area should be minimized insofar as this is possible. To insure that even a random encounter with the form will not result in discomfort, avoid the use of sharp corners and edges except where the form rests on the table.

Extrinsic Forces

Size, shape, texture, and character of human hand, direction and magnitude of forces to be supported, and minimization of bulk and surface area.

Intrinsic Forces

Characteristics and limitations of materials, and fabrication techniques and skills.

Performance Standards

This problem does not allow for strict quantitative performance measurements, but it can be clearly evaluated by testing. Optimum performance is achieved when people with many different sizes and shapes of hands use the form for leaning and all agree that it is comfortable.

Techniques and Materials

Various approaches may be taken for the fabrication of the table leaner. Rigid plastic foam is perhaps the easiest material to shape, but it is difficult to finish. A soft wood such as clear pine, or even balsa, may also be used. Shaping the wood by carving is more difficult than shaping foam, but the wood is usually easier to finish and works very well.

It is desirable that the completed form have a smooth, slick automobile-type painted finish. This can be accomplished in foam as follows: Develop and perfect the shape by carving, sawing, rasping, and sanding. When the shape cannot be improved anymore, fill the entire surface with premixed

28 in.
(71 cm.)

patching plaster (Spackle). After the coating has thoroughly dried, sand carefully. Repeat the spackling and sanding process until there are no more flaws in the surface. Sand with fine garnet or sandpaper.

Before painting, seal the surface with a clear sealer that is compatible with the paint to be used for the final finish. More than one coat of sealer may be required. Paint with an aerosol spray paint. The type of paint that is used for wood models works particularly well.

Wood can be fashioned and finished in a manner similar to foam. After carving and filling, a great deal of sanding from coarse to fine is required to get a good, smooth finish. Only after the wood is sanded quite smooth should the sanding sealer be used. Two or three coats of sealer is best with fine sanding between each coat and before paint is applied. Use of Spackle is usually unnecessary if sanding has been done carefully and a high-quality sanding sealer is used. A more ambitious under-taking would be to carve the table leaner from hardwood and use a transparent lacquer or similar finish.

Conceptual Guidelines

The most important principle in the solution to this problem is that the form should not become too specific. That is, it should not fit just one particular hand. A more generalized form usually works best for everyone. The shape of the form will govern the angle at which the hand and wrist are disposed when leaning on the table, so this should be considered carefully, since it can impact critically on the comfort of the hand-support form.

The requirement that excessive bulk and surface area be minimized comes into play only after the basic shape has been established by consideration of the appropriate extrinsic forces. The elimination of excessive bulk is straightforward and one can readily intuit a close approximation of a minimized surface area. An approximation will have to suffice since actual surface area calculations are extraordinarily difficult and beyond the scope and need of our present concerns. The avoidance of sharp corners and edges actually follows directly from the minimization of surface area. Therefore, to eliminate corners and edges is to further minimize surface area. In any case, the form evolves to a relatively perfected state by the careful attention to all of these extrinsic forces.

This problem serves as an introduction to ergonomic design, which, when properly considered, is always a diagram of forces. Think through the shape carefully and avoid arbitrary decisions as much as possible. Always look for possible forces or influences that could determine the form. We are not suggesting that the world needs a table leaner, but this problem serves as a useful exercise by calling attention to certain kinds of considerations in the evolution or creation of built form.

Chapter 2:
Problem Solutions

Solutions: Problem 1. Paper Tower

Seven different typical solutions to Problem 1A and B, paper tower, are shown. Side views, or elevations [2.1a] and corresponding end views [2.1b] are included. Note that the performance capability of these columnar structures is determined by their cross-sectional configuration. There are a variety of possible cross-sectional configurations. Some will be better than others, but a surprising number will yield virtually equivalent strength-to-weight ratios. A simple cylindrical tubular column (not shown) will form a structure that is difficult to improve upon. Fluted cylinders can also work very well.

The bulging tower on the far left has no particular advantage, and, in fact, tends to suffer from unnecessary complication. Since the stress induced by the applied load is unidirectional, there is no need to deviate from a simple straight-sided, tubular structure. Structures of the type shown on the left tend to fail at the points where the surfaces change direction, since stress is typically concentrated at these points.

In [2.2a-c] an 18-inch-high paper tower is gradually loaded with bricks until it collapses. Approximately 24 pounds were required to cause this structure to fail—a good performance. Uniformity in construction is extremely important with these paper towers, since failure will always occur first where constructional flaws exist. For this reason, it is often useful to design column cross-sections as combinations of flat planes (third from right [2.1b], rather than arced surfaces (second from right [2.1b]. Two flat surfaces may be easily joined without appreciable distortion—an accomplishment difficult to achieve when attempting to join adjacent arced surfaces.

Since the "force" to be "diagrammed" in this problem is only vertically directed, the form options are straightforward and relatively limited. Developing a solution of optimum performance, however, is a fruitful learning experience that not only leads to a surprising diversity of cross-sectional configurations but serves as a good introduction to the problems that follow.

18

2.1a

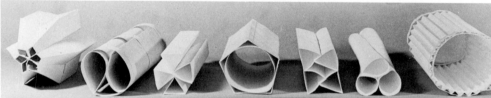

2.1b

2.2a

2.2b

2.2c

2.3

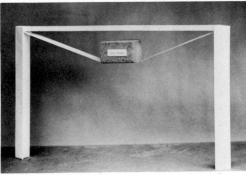

2.4

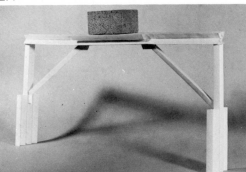

2.5

2.6

Solutions: Problem 2. Paper Bridge

Ten different solutions to Problem 2, paper bridge, are shown. The substantial increase in complexity of this problem compared to the paper tower manifests itself in the corresponding increase in the diversity of possible solutions. The distribution of the concentrated load of 6 pounds can become quite circuitous and complex. The task is to find the simplest, most direct route of stress distribution by deftly employing the essential principles of structural behavior and materials properties.

In [2.3] is a classic post and lintel (column and beam) system. As pervasive as this structure is in the built environment, of all solutions illustrated here, it is markedly less efficient than any of the others. It works, but its strength-to-weight ratio is very poor.

Figure [2.4] is a structure which, at first glance, also appears to be a post and lintel structure. Nothing could be further from the truth. Like [2.3], each of the vertical columns of [2.4] must support half the total applied weight—3 pounds. However, unlike [2.3], the horizontal component of [2.4] does not function as a beam at all. Indeed, it demonstrates a brilliant understanding of the principles of structure. Specifically, the functions of tension and compression are differentiated in such a way that the horizontal member is loaded in pure compression as an ideal column by means of a tension sling to which the load is applied. No bending loads are to be found anywhere in the structure. As a result, the components can have their weights reduced to a minimum.

Figure [2.5] is another variation on a post and lintel system, nicely executed, but only slightly more efficient than the structure in [2.3]. Its increase in efficiency is due to the addition of inclined side supports that contribute to the shortening of the effective span of the horizontal beam. Actually this kind of bracing of a post and beam structure has more value in the restraint of lateral loads, such as wind loads, which are not relevant to the current problem.

Another remarkably efficient structure is shown in [2.6]. This structure, a variation of [2.4], has an additional short vertical compression member wedged between the applied load and the horizontal

20

2.7

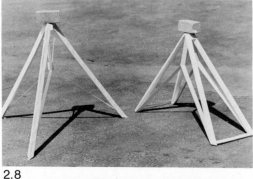

2.8

2.9

compression member. This has the effect of reducing the horizontal compression member to half of its original length with respect to its ability to resist stress. Since a shorter, thicker column will support more weight than a longer, thinner one, we can see why this structure would exceed even [2.4] in efficiency.

In [2.7] is yet another variation on the principle of differentiating the functions of tension and compression. In this case, the tension member is horizontal, and the compression member is translated into two inclined components meeting at a common apex where the load is applied. Although, in this example, these inclined members are unnecessarily long, it is nonetheless an efficient structure.

In [2.8] and [2.9] are shown four structures which, to varying degrees, take advantage of the principle of differentiating the functions of tension and compression in their structural components. There are no bending loads induced anywhere in any of these structures; that is, no beams occur. The foreground structure in [2.9] is likely to be just about optimally efficient relative to strength-to-weight since the compression members are about as short as they can get. This is made possible by the effective integration of the tension members into the structure.

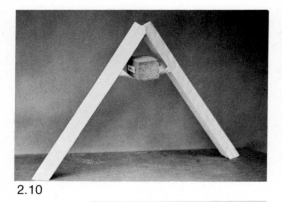

2.10

2.11

The implications of not differentiating the functions of tension and compression in this paper bridge problem can be appreciated by carefully considering [2.10] and [2.11]. In [2.10] a short tension sling supports the applied load but connects to the inclined support members at an intermediate point, which induces a direct bending load to these compression members causing them to function as beams. The result is that the support members have to be appropriately reinforced thus adding to the weight of the structure and reducing the structural efficiency. This apparently simple structure becomes a system in which very indirect and complex stress distribution takes place. In the final analysis, this structure is an improvement over the simple post and beam, but only by a slight amount as it ranks near the bottom in strength-to-weight relative to the other examples shown.

Likewise, [2.11] is not particularly efficient since it also fails to clearly differentiate the functions of tension and compression. It is substantially more efficient that [2.10], however, since the tension members meet the compression members at oblique angles thereby distributing some of the stress into the member as compression. In [2.10] the tension member loads the support member at approximately 90°, which causes all the stress to be induced as bending.

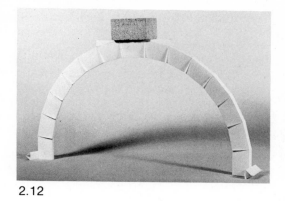

2.12

One may wonder about the relevance of the ubiquitous arch that was so prominent in the early history of building. Traditionally and originally, the arch was a structural form that was a gravity-oriented system. That is, it is an almost totally pure compression structure built of stone. To function efficiently a classic arch needs to be securely fastened at its footings to prevent its base from spreading. Since, in the present problem, the structure may be neither tied across the bottom, nor, what is the same thing, fastened to a base, the classic arch is not a particularly viable strategy.

Figure [2.12] is a classic arch beautifully constructed from paper. Although this structure would hold some weight, it could not hold the required 6 pounds. It could be made to do so, but only with a considerable weight penalty. Since an arch is nothing but a section from a polygon, one can hypothesize an arch that has fewer sides and that may, indeed, even differentiate tension from compression. In fact, the foreground structure in [2.9] is such a fundamental arch system. So we see that even the arch, when correctly interpreted for the problem and materials at hand, can have an important role in the solution to the paper bridge problem.

The ten examples shown in [2.3] through [2.12] represent a range of possible solutions. There are as many solutions as there are people to work on the problem. Just remember that those few really good performing structures are the ones in which one's undivided attention has been focused on the intrinsic forces of the properties of the material and of the general principles of structure.

Solutions: Problem 3. Stick Tower

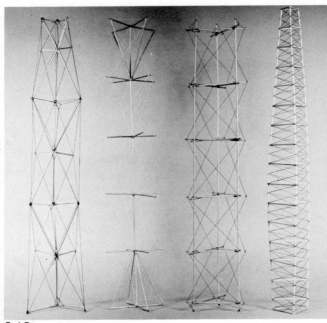

2.13

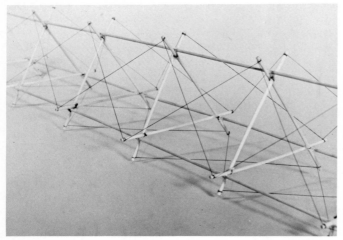

2.14

In [2.13] are shown four solutions to Problem 3, the stick tower. Theoretically, the most efficient design should be the tower second from left. In this particular embodiment, however, it did not quite work, though presumably this masting system with its tensionally braced single compression member or spine could be made to work. The principle demonstrated here is that of converting the long (30-inch) flexible ⅛-inch dowel (spine) to a series of short rigid compression members that are supported by intermittent horizontal compression members or ribs. The ribs are fixed in position by a series of carefully positioned tension lines. In the example shown, two horizontal sticks form 90° crosses at vertical intervals of 6 inches. To make this system work would probably require three horizontal sticks crossing at 60° angles at vertical intervals of 5 inches. In so doing, more weight is added with a corresponding decrease in efficiency. If it would work, however, it probably would turn out to be a good performer from the standpoint of strength-to-weight. •

The structure on the left in [2.13] is also a marginal performer as it was barely able to support 8 pounds. It is a structure of some merit, however, with potential high strength-to-weight. Like the braced single-stick tower discussed above, it consists of a series of tripods alternately inverted. Tension members are used to prevent the ends of the tripod from spreading apart. Both structures on the left suffer from too much overall flexibility. They tend to sway excessively under load, causing the tower to eventually tip over rather than break.

The structure on the right is quite strong and readily supports the required weight of 8 pounds. It is somewhat excessive in its use of material, however, as it has far more horizontal struts than are really required. The structure second from the right proved to be the most successful. It is quite strong and relatively efficient in terms of its strength-to-weight ratio. It is well-made and carefully detailed [2.14], and the connections are deftly executed. Essentially a triangular prism, it consists of three vertical main spars, a vertical succession of horizontal triangular frames, and two-way diagonal bracing with the tension members (string). The diagonal bracing is a form of triangulation and is necessary to give the tower adequate stiffness. The geometry of a rectangular frame is inherently unstable, and the most efficient way to stabilize such a frame is with diagonal bracing. If such bracing is done with tension members, it must be a two-way arrangement, so-called "X" bracing. If the bracing is a compression member, with tensile capability, a single diagonal will suffice. This principle can be easily verified by simple experiment. With varying degrees of success, all four structures attempt to take advantage of the principle of triangulation. It is the only way to insure geometric stability in such structures and, therefore, the only way to achieve adequate strength.

Figure [2.15] is a tower assembled entirely from equal length short struts forming a fully triangulated structure of enormous strength. The equilateral triangles combine to provide a structure of complete geometric stability. This particular example will support a load far in excess of the required 8 pounds—perhaps as much as 20 pounds. It is very efficient in terms of strength-to-weight, but is actually stronger than is necessary to solve Problem 3. It might be possible to reduce its weight by substituting tension members for some of the compression members, but this would have to be done with great care to preserve the integrity of the system. It could be made in the same configuration with lighter weight, thinner struts, but this would take it outside the requirements of the problem, i.e., ⅛-inch dowels. In any case, this tower constitutes a fundamental structure and is a good frame of reference.

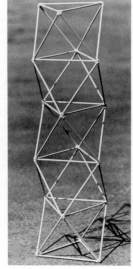

2.15

If a tower were built as a stacking of cubes, with the same weight as the triangulated tower, its performance would be substantially inferior to its counterpart of triangles, even with strong and rigid connections. It would also have only approximately half the load capacity. This simple direct comparison clearly demonstrates the advantage of triangulated systems relative to strength-to-weight.

Solutions: Problem 4. Stick Bridge

Like the paper bridge, the stick bridge is a problem of some complexity. Since it uses compact materials of relatively high compressive and tensile strength, it is a problem that can give rise to a great diversity of structural solutions. Even more diversity is possible than is the case with the paper bridge problem. We show here in [2.16] through [2.28], thirteen possible solutions. The careful observer will note some structural themes that have appeared in solutions to the paper bridge, and others which bear little resemblance to such arrangements of paper.

2.16

In [2.16] is a structure that appears to be a simple post and beam system. However, in a form virtually identical to some of the paper bridges [2.4], the forces of tension and compression are quite clearly and usefully differentiated. Once again, the given weight is supported by a tension sling that is loaded into the ends of the horizontal beam-like compression members, the ends of which are supported equally by simple columns. These columns, including the horizontal one, consist of rectangular-framed triangular prisms that are stabilized by tension member X-bracing. This moderately efficient bridge works well and is precisely made. It is certainly much more efficient than would be a comparable post and beam structure.

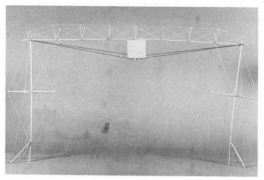

2.17

Figure [2.17] is a substantial improvement over the structure in [2.16]. It is essentially the same principle as in [2.16]—two vertical columns supporting a horizontal component that is loaded in pure compression by means of load-supporting tension sling. This improved structure, however, is approximately one-third the weight of [2.16], a difference that can be readily observed in the photos. Compare the braced single-stick vertical supports of [2.17] with the triple vertical sticks of the support columns in [2.16], and compare the respective horizontal components.

In [2.17] the horizontal compression member is reduced to an absolute minimum. A single long spinal dowel is braced by a combination of short compression members, or ribs, and tension elements. This horizontal component is preloaded by wedging the weight (brick) between the dowel spine and the tension support sling. When this is done, the tension members, which stabilize the long dowel spine, become tight and function with optimum efficiency. It is difficult to imagine a more efficient interpretation of this particular generic solution.

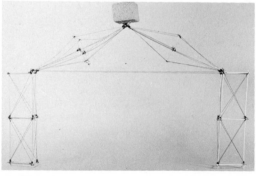

2.18

In [2.18] can be seen what might be considered another generic solution. Remember that we have already seen an interpretation of this arrangement in paper [2.7]. It is a variation of [2.16] and [2.17] insofar as it consists of major structural components that clearly differentiate the functions of tension and compression. Its essentially horizontal tension/compression support system is held at the appropriate height with two vertical support columns. The difference from [2.16] and [2.17] is readily apparent. The weight is supported at the apex of two adjoining inclined compression members. The stability of the compression members is guaranteed by the horizontal tension member that resists the tendency for these compression members to spread apart. This particular structure is relatively efficient, falling somewhere between [2.16] and [2.17]. Note that there is a certain untidiness in execution and that some improvement in efficiency could be anticipated through refinement of design. Nonetheless, [2.18] is a structure based on sound principles.

In the evolution of a highly sophisticated solution to this stick bridge problem, optimum efficiency will be achieved when every ounce of material is directed toward the sole purpose of supporting the required load—that is, all structural members are working. When loaded, the tension members are tensed, and the compression members are compressed. In a structural arrangement such behavior can be experimentally demonstrated and verified through careful observation. The structures in [2.19] and [2.20] exhibit this level of optimization. It is difficult to imagine solutions to this problem of any greater efficiency.

The structure in [2.19] shows an extraordinarily purposeful use of tension members that allow the compression member components to be reduced to an absolute minimum. A single spine horizontal beam member is made short in length by the use of inclined triangular support frames or columns. A carefully organized network of tension strands maintains the stability of the entire assembly. Curiously, this structure should properly be considered an interpretation of a post and beam system, although it strays far from a pure post and beam arrangement.

Similarly, [2.20] could be considered a derivation of an arch. Like [2.19], it is a structure in which every component works when it is loaded. Note how the tension members are joined at a common point under the frame supporting the brick, and observe how the support frame under the brick is designed to just fit the brick. The bowed, two-stick compression members on each side are preloaded by the tension members thereby taking advantage of the elastic properties of the wood dowel. The weight of the brick in this structure is quite clearly transmitted directly down each side of the structure—an almost perfect expression of form as a diagram of forces. Good detailing and craftsmanship is evident in both structures, serving the high level of performance very well.

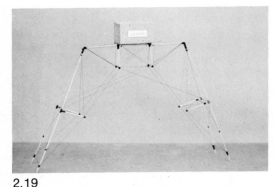

2.19

2.20

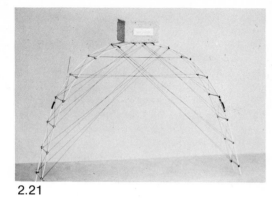

2.21

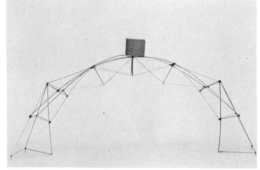

2.22

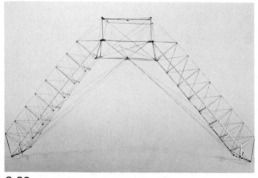

2.23

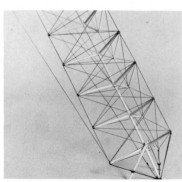

2.24

A more literal demonstration of the arch is shown in [2.21]. This example is reasonably efficient, but it uses more material than [2.20], is less clearly thought through, less carefully constructed, and simply not as strong. In spite of these deficiencies, it is a substantially better performer than a number of other possible solutions.

In [2.22] is another interpretation of an arch that is quite interesting, but relatively inefficient. It is reasonably coherent as a structure in the sense that most of the material used is purposeful. It simply uses more material than it needs to in order to do the job. Also it is not particularly strong, in an absolute sense, being rather unstable through the upper arch region.

Figure [2.23] is another solution of good efficiency. It is not quite as light as [2.19] or [2.20], but is nonetheless among the better performing structures. It consists of two inclined single spine columns joined at the top by a very short horizontal structure. Although not shown in the photograph, the design presumes that the applied load would rest on the compression members that define the highest points on the bridge on each side of the center of the structure. These compression members, in turn, transfer the load directly to the spines of each of the two inclined support columns, which become loaded in pure compression. Long tension members keep the inclined compression members from spreading. Although there is some redundancy in the inclined columns, they are extraordinarily well executed [2.24], with flawless craftsmanship and clearly thought-out and assembled networks of tension and compression members.

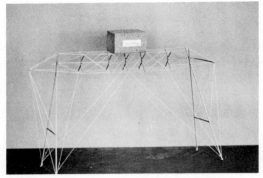

2.25

2.26

2.27

Another spinal structure is seen in [2.25]. It is relatively simple, lightweight, and beautifully executed but incorporates the braced single spine component in a nonoptimum manner. In this instance, the braced spine is loaded in direct bending as a beam, rather than in pure compression as a column—the manner in which such structural components should be loaded. On the top side of the spinal beam, the tension members all go limp as the beam deflects under load, while only the tension members on the lower side are doing any work. Compare this structure to that of [2.19] in which a single spine beam is effectively developed. All secondary support components, tension and compression, are on the bottom side of the beam where they are put to work as the load is applied and the spine deflects.

Although a bit inefficient, the tripod structure in [2.26] exhibits an effective use of braced spinal columns that are loaded in pure compression. The applied load is clearly transferred directly into the three legs of the tripod, with long tension members used to prevent the legs of the tripod from spreading. Note that these tension supports are connected to nodal points along the spine, as well as at the ends, to distribute the stress and to minimize bending loads on the spine. Such bending loads will inevitably upset the sought-after condition of pure compression in the long spinal components.

In [2.27] and [2.28] can be seen two straightforward post and beam structures. Both are neatly executed and reasonably well thought out. The structure in [2.27] is quite strong, actually too strong since it is unnecessarily heavy. The horizontal beam spans a full 24 inches and has a stiffness because of its depth, which far exceeds the capacity of the columns that support it. The two inclined stick braces, which go from the lower center of the beam to a lower stick brace on the columns, control any instability or flexing that may occur in the columns. However, they constitute an inefficient solution to such problems.

2.28

In [2.28] is a more reasonable approach to such a problem. In this case, the columns are tilted outwardly at the bottom to insure that any instability would manifest itself as a tendency for the columns to spread apart. This is quite significant because a simple system of tension members will provide the necessary stability. Also, the inclined columns enable the span of the beam to be reduced, thereby enabling it to be lighter and stronger. In fact, among the examples we have shown, [2.28] is a relatively good performing structure, although it definitely does not approach the elegant efficiency of [2.19] and [2.20].

We have shown thirteen examples of solutions to the stick bridge problem. The linear character of the material properties of button thread and wood dowels enables forces to be diagrammed rather directly. Preparatory investigations can lead to an understanding of fundamental principles that can be turned to considerable advantage in the solution of the stick bridge problem. Each example we have shown has some sound structural principles included in its design—otherwise it would not work at all. There is a surprising range of efficiency, from elegantly light and strong structures to very heavy structures that barely work at all. Even among those that exhibit optimum efficiency, there is a great diversity of possible solutions. Remember that none of the solutions, even the most sophisticated structures, were done by professionals. They were all made by college freshmen, male and female. As we pointed out with the paper bridge problem, the brilliantly performing solutions are those in which the general principles of structure are completely integrated with the intrinsic properties (forces) of the prescribed materials by means of a relentlessly careful empiricism.

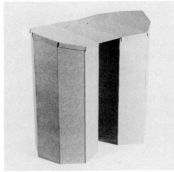

2.29a

2.29b

2.30a

2.30b

Solutions: Problem 5. Cardboard Stool

The cardboard stool problem is essentially an extension of the paper tower problem. The materials are somewhat the same, and the location of the applied load is similar. On the other hand, the applied load is a so-called "live load" and presents a decidedly more complex problem of stress distribution than does the simple concentrated brick load of the paper tower. The cardboard itself is quite similar in its properties to the paper used in the paper tower problem, and some of the problems learned from the paper tower can be directly applied to this problem though there are differences between the two.

Thirteen different solutions to the cardboard stool problem are shown. Once again, a surprising diversity of possible solutions is seen—some quite efficient and others unnecessarily heavy. In [2.29a-b] is one of the most efficient stools weighing only 18.5 ounces. It is quite straightforward in its concept and carefully executed with good attention to details. It is also one of the most comfortable stools to sit on. Notice how the seat area is contoured while being successfully integrated into the structure of the stool. Also observe that the cardboard is treated as a series of flat planes that are precisely folded to form a closed polygonal structure of great stiffness, and that the folds in the seat exactly match the folds in the vertical structure. This stool will hold barely more than the prescribed 180 pounds, but it does convincingly support that required minimum weight.

In [2.30a-b] is another efficient solution that weighs about the same as [2.29], although, with its small flat seat, it is not quite as comfortable. It is fairly well constructed consisting of three tapering columns that are nicely connected to each other along common vertical edges. One effective detail is the manner in which the seat is tied into the three columns. Three symmetrically opposed (triangular symmetry) flaps are folded down from the seat plane to fit obliquely onto the vertical surfaces of the columns. These flaps stiffen and support the seat and transfer some of the seat load into the columns. The tapered columns reduce the area of the base support, which tends to increase the stool's tendency to tip when loaded. Such tapering, however, also reduces the surface area of the columns and, therefore, the weight of the structure.

2.31

2.32

2.33a

2.33b

Another rather lightweight stool—18.5 ounces— is shown in [2.31]. A simple cardboard cylinder is braced three-dimensionally by an internal folded cardboard structure. This intriguing solution presented a difficult problem of connecting the inner structure to the outer cylinder. The connections could only be made at a series of points, and they inevitably tended to fail. Presumably, this would be a solvable problem but was nonetheless troublesome.

In [2.32] and [2.33a–b] can be seen two solutions that provided a great deal of strength. This strength, however, is at the expense of increased weight of 24 ounces, but both solutions are of more than passing interest. Figure [2.32] is a collection of eight triangular columns organized in pairs around a central square. This example is rather poorly made and is constructed of heavier material than is necessary. The seat, in particular, exhibits a lack of attention to detail with its unsupported overhangs and sharp corners. It is a concept, however, that could yield a very good performing solution.

In [2.33a–b] can be seen a relatively complex, but intriguing, solution. It is constructed of relatively thin cardboard and is enormously strong. The fluted column, looking much like an eight-sided asterisk in cross-section, is stabilized by three horizontal disks that fit into appropriate slots in the column. A central vertical cylinder offers additional support to the seat. It is not known whether this concept could be developed with even thinner cardboard to get the weight down close to 18 ounces. Given the relatively high strength of this structure, however, it seems likely that a lighter version could be made that would be capable of supporting 180 pounds.

2.34

Figure [2.34] is an interesting variation on a fluted column structure. In this case, a very light—14 ounces—structure was built, but it did not successfully support 180 pounds. The column is an eight-pointed star in cross-section and is a full 15 inches high. It is capped, top and bottom, by octagonal boxes that are neatly integrated into the columns. These boxes provide base support and seat surface as well as acting to stabilize the fluted column. This stool could undoubtedly be made to work, but at what cost in weight is uncertain.

Three variations on an "hourglass" or double cone shape can be seen in [2.35], [2.36], and [2.37]. Two truncated octagonal pyramid structures are joined end for end in [2.35a–b]. When carefully executed, as this example is, it can work very well. Note the carefully detailed seat. Although some strength can be lost compared to a simple columnar structure, the hourglass shape definitely reduces the total surface area and, therefore, the weight of the structure. This shape also tends to differentiate stresses more than does a simple column. The base and seat area are generally loaded in tension while the joined ends are loaded in compression.

In [2.36a–b] is a beautifully detailed and constructed structure consisting of two opposed truncated cones joined at their apices and reinforced by a central cylinder. Note the very nice detailing of the connections where the cones meet each other inside the cylinder and where the seat joins the outer edge at the top. Also note the double wall reinforcement at the base ring. At 13.5 ounces, this structure was very light, but it was subject to some buckling where the lowest edge of the cylinder meets the cone. Reinforcement at that region would be required before the structure would be readily able to support 180 pounds.

In [2.37a–b] can be seen yet another variation of novel construction, on the hourglass theme. This structure is quite strong, easily supporting the required weight of 180 pounds. However, it was also relatively heavy since the overlapping surfaces of the cardboard strips added to the total amount of material used. The unique tension strap seat and its virtual compound surface were quite effective. Once again, this is a concept which, with lighter-weight material, might be amenable to substantial weight reduction.

2.35a

2.35b

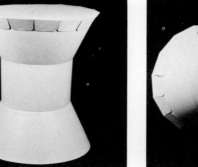

2.36a

2.36b

2.37a

2.37b

Four additional solutions are shown in [2.38] through [2.41]. Figure [2.38] is a converging elliptical column in which a tension seat system is supported by a compression ring at the top of the column. This comfortable stool worked well and was only moderately heavy. In [2.39] is another departure that looks more like a conventional stool structure with four legs. Each leg is a tapering triangular column nicely integrated into the seat with tension members preventing the legs from spreading at the base when under load. This stool was quite comfortable and very strong. Its weight was somewhat disappointing, however, at 24 ounces.

A rather heavyweight stool—32 ounces—is seen in [2.40]. It is one of enormous strength, however. It consists of a hexagonal column in which the interior is subdivided into an array of triangular sub-columns. Great strength would be anticipated from such a system. With more careful attention to size and weight of material, an efficient interpretation of this concept could no doubt be developed. Finally, a rather heavy stool at 31.5 ounces is shown in [2.41] Once again, we see an interesting concept that is relatively poorly thought through and executed. A central triangular column is augmented by three outer support structures of an interesting configuration providing an effective mode of stress distribution.

As in the four previous structure problems, a great diversity of solutions seems possible. It is clear that careful attention to details, good craftsmanship, and sensitive observation of structural behavior are the keys to arriving at and successfully executing a good performing structure. Beyond that, a certain amount of invention can always help one strive toward the exquisite diagram of forces so eloquently displayed time and time again in the natural world.

2.38a

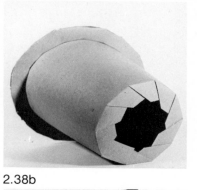

2.38b

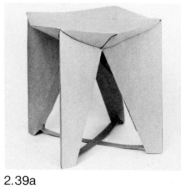

2.39a

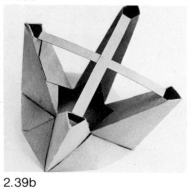

2.39b

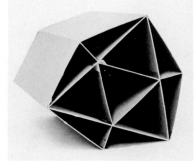

2.40

2.41a

2.41b

Solutions: Problem 6. Table Leaner

Four distinctly different, but successful, solutions to the table leaner problem are shown in [2.42] through [2.45]. Each form is shown with a hand in place and in approximately the same view without the hand. The angle of contact is slightly different in each form. In [2.42] the hand is nearly horizontal requiring a bend in the wrist to point the arm in the proper direction, while in [2.45], the hand and arm are nearly on the same axis thereby minimizing the angle in the wrist. Both solutions have their advantages and disadvantages, but both quite successfully deal with their respective geometries.

All four examples actually work quite well and exhibit a high degree of sophistication and refinement in their forms. Notice the generalized, but quite subtle, form of each solution, and observe how each form eliminates excessive bulk and minimizes surface area in a manner appropriate to its particular overall shape. Indeed, since this kind of problem does not conveniently lend itself to the kind of quantitative scrutiny applicable to the structural performance evaluation of Problems 1–5, the concept of appropriateness becomes the essential element in the pursuit of perfection of form. With form as diagram of forces as the fundamental conceptual guideline, one must often rely in the design of built form on what Charles Eames called the "smell for appropriateness." The table leaner provides an opportunity, within the context of a relatively simple problem, to come to grips with this sense of appropriateness.

2.42a

2.42b

2.43a

2.43b

2.44a

2.44b

2.45a

2.45b

Part II
The Structure of Form:
An Integrated Experience

Chapter 3:
The Evolution of a Form

Problem 1: Random Assembly of Cubes

3.1a

3.1b

Problem

Create a random assembly of thirty equal-sized cubes [3.1a-b]. The assembly is to be as asymmetrical as possible, but must have three equally spaced cubes on a common base plane. The three base cubes must be the lowest cubes in the structure. No other cubes must be on or below the base plane.

A fourth cube is to be placed vertically above the center of the triangle formed by the base cubes. This fourth cube must be the highest cube in the assembly, but otherwise may be positioned at an arbitrary height.

Assuming a recommended dimension of 1.5 inches (3.8 cm) per cube, the entire assembly must fit within the boundaries of an imaginary 14-inch (35.6 cm) sphere. All cubes in the assembly must be parallel and may be joined only on their faces.

Within the limitations outlined above, the configuration of the cube assembly can be quite arbitrary. The primary purpose of this problem is to provide a vehicle for the problems which are to follow.

Extrinsic Forces

Design objectives and dimensional constraints.

Intrinsic Forces

Geometric and symmetry properties of the cube, the nature of three-dimensional space, properties of materials, and quality of construction.

Conceptual Guidelines

Within the dimensional parameters given, the criterion of maximum asymmetry is open to some interpretation. Relative degrees of symmetry can be objectively analyzed and can be exactly ranked. In addition, the point where a configuration no longer has any symmetry can be precisely established. (See *Polyhedra Primer*, pages 14–18.) Degrees of asymmetry, on the other hand, cannot be clearly ranked. Nonetheless, when comparing different assymmetrical forms, a consensus can usually be reached as to which is more asymmetrical.

44

3.2

Techniques and Materials

The recommended 1.5-inch (3.8 cm) cubes can be fabricated nicely from clear pine or other kinds of soft or hard wood. In the USA, clear pine is typically available in ¾-inch thick (1.9 cm) boards of various widths. Using white glue, laminate two boards together to create a board of approximately 1.5-inch thickness (3.8 cm). Carefully measure the actual thickness of the laminated board, and then with a table saw or radial arm saw, cut cubic blocks whose sides are exactly the thickness of the laminated board, i.e., 1.5 × 1.5 × 1.5 inches (3.8 × 3.8 × 3.8 cm). Cut 30 of these cubes.

It is useful to construct the cube assembly upon a baseboard of some kind [3.2]. Quarter-inch (6.3 mm) Masonite or plastic works well. As the structure is assembled, use a combination square against the baseboard to check the vertical alignment of the cubes. Establish the relative positions of the three equally spaced base cubes on the baseboard. Ideally, these three cubes should be anchored to the baseboard by small pegs or dowels. This allows the assembly to be lifted off the board for a subsequent step in this problem sequence. Carefully assemble the structure from the base cubes insuring that all cubes remain parallel to each other in all respects.

Use glue sparingly so that changes can be made as the structure is built. A faster drying glue, such as aliphatic resin white glue or model airplane cement for wood, may be preferable to regular white glue, which has a very slow drying time.

Problem 2: Minimum-Maximum Envelope

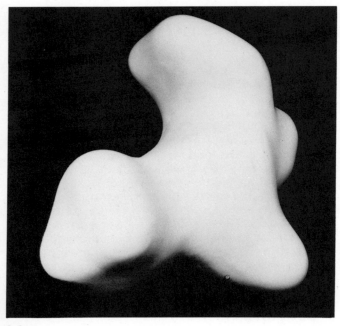

3.3a

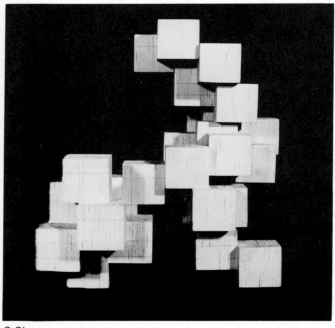

3.3b

Problem

Design and perfect the form of a homogeneous envelope that will exactly enclose the random cube assembly. The form must equally satisfy the seemingly contradictory criteria of minimized or least surface area and of greatest distribution of stress. A continuously flowing form is to be created in which no sudden changes in direction are exhibited, and in which all extraneous surface area is eliminated. A typical form and its related random cube assembly are shown in [3.3a-b].

Extrinsic Forces

Configuration of the random assembly of cubes.

Intrinsic Forces

Natural principles of minimized surface area and maximized distribution of stress; techniques and materials used.

Conceptual Guidelines

We can assume that the random assembly of cubes is an architectural metaphor, which represents a collection of functional, social and aesthetic parameters. It becomes a three-dimensional spatial diagram of extrinsic forces and design constraints. The principles of minimized surface area and maximized distribution of stress are viewed as natural phenomena and as such are considered intrinsic forces.

The notion of minimum surface area can only be understood relative to some frame of reference. The classic model for minimal surfaces in nature is the soap film in its many variations. A single soap bubble is spherical because when it assumes such a shape, its surface relative to its volume is minimized and its stresses are equally distributed.

The single bubble exactly satisfies our criteria of minimized surface and maximum distribution of stress. Its minimized surface, however, is relative to volume instead of relative to a form of predetermined configuration. If the soap bubble could somehow be distorted to correspond to our random cube assembly it would most likely take the form of the minimum-maximum envelope.

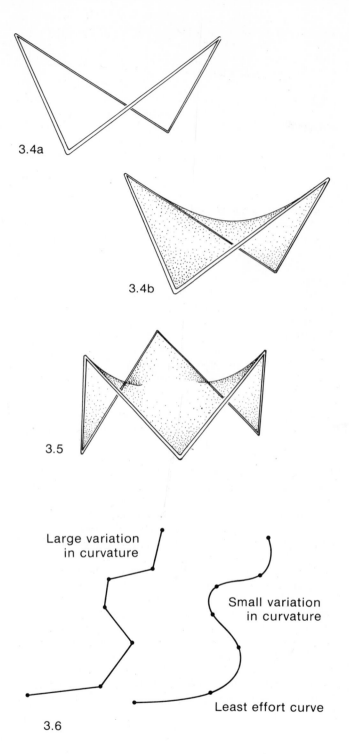

3.4a

3.4b

3.5

Large variation
in curvature

Small variation
in curvature

Least effort curve

3.6

In a froth of bubbles [5.3], surface-to-volume is once again minimized, but the array of bubbles must assume the shapes of various closely packed polyhedra, which share faces with their neighbors. These shared faces often exhibit a saddle-like curvature.

When a wire frame polygon [3.4a] is immersed in a soap solution and then removed, a thin film of soap is deposited by spanning the frame [3.4b]. Such a film is the membrane of least surface area that will completely span the frame, and it is usually referred to as a minimal surface.

When the polygon is flat, the minimal surface will be a flat plane. When the polygon is not flat, however, the minimal surface will be a saddle shape of some kind. Such non-flat polygons are called skew polygons. It makes no difference how many sides the polygon has, since the soap will conform to any configuration. The simplest skew polygon has four sides and its minimal surface is a simple single saddle. Skew polygons with greater numbers of sides generate compound saddle shapes of intriguing complexity [3.5].

The form of the homogeneous envelope will approximate a three-dimensional array of saddle-like forms connected together. Since these hypothetical saddle forms are not actually derived from finite polygons, there will be no clear boundaries between them. The result is a fluidity of form that exemplifies a principle of continuity. Such a principle is an important one in natural structure (see river meander, [5.10]), and leads us to the other design objective for the minimum-maximum envelope.

If minimized surface was the only design objective of the homogenous envelope, then the cubes would press out against the envelope at its extremities. Since, however, maximized distribution of stress is also a design objective, variation in curvature must also be minimized. This means that the form must consist of curves in which change of direction must be distributed over the greatest possible distance [3.6]. Under these conditions, curves of least effort are created in which stress is equally and optimally distributed. In other words, the minimum-maximum envelope must be a form that is gentle in its continuous transitions from one surface orientation to another. This required continuity results in a form in which the underlying cubic array does not make its presence known even at the extremities of the form.

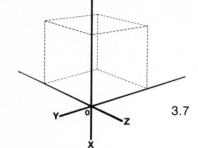

3.7

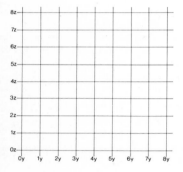

x plane

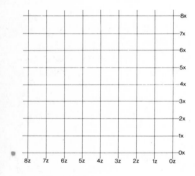

y plane

z plane

3.8a

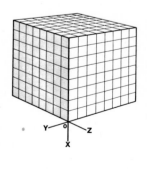

3.8b

Since the minimal surfaces of skew polygons already represent arrangements of least energy, the integration of minimized surface and maximized stress distribution is readily achieved. In practical terms, there is no easy and convenient way to rigorously evolve a minimum-maximum envelope that is mathematically perfected. It is possible, however, through disciplined intuition and careful methodology to evolve a form in which the intrinsic logic provides a convincing approximation of a minimum-maximum envelope.

Techniques and Materials

There are always a variety of methods that can be used to solve problems of the sort outlined above. One approach is to simply sculpt from a large block of plaster, wood, or rigid plastic foam a form that seems to characterize the sought-after attributes. Even a skilled and experienced sculptor with highly developed spatial sensibilities would benefit, however, from the use of some techniques that would increase the accuracy of his or her efforts. A methodology has been evolved that is within the technical capabilities of a relatively inexperienced student and that gives some assurance that a solution will be fashioned which adequately fulfills the objectives of the problem. It is also a methodology that teaches skills of general usefulness to anyone aspiring to be a designer or architect.

The methodology involves the creation of an "egg crate" model that describes the contours of the minimum-maximum envelope. Development of the egg crate model begins with a three-dimensional analysis of the random cube array. Cross-sections of the cube array must be established at many horizontal and vertical planes of reference. This is achieved through the use of a three-dimensional x,y,z coordinate system [3.7].

Such a system is defined by three sets of grid planes [3.8a] that are keyed in a three-dimensional relationship to a common point of reference or zero point [3.8b]. In effect, the grid for a three-dimensional graph is created. The x plane is established as the base plane. A convenient grid to use is 1.5 inches (3.8 cm).

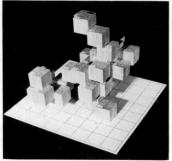

3.9

3.10a

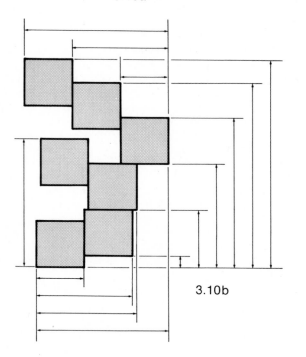

3.10b

Lay out such a grid on heavy white paper and mount it to the baseboard of the previously constructed cube assembly. Mount the cube array on the baseboard [3.9]. The number of units in the grid should correspond to the size of the structure, with room to spare. The example shown requires an 8-unit grid. The position of the cube structure is somewhat arbitrary as long as it is generally centered on the grid. It must be oriented, however, so that the cube faces are parallel to the grid. One useful procedure is to align the cube assembly so that some of the cube faces within the structure align with the grid exactly.

The lines on the base or x plane represent the positions of the vertical y and z planes. Some of these vertical planes will intersect certain cubes within the assembly. These planes of intersection of the cube assembly are cross-sections.

Cross-sections are created by carefully measuring the locations of particular cubes which fall in given grid planes. This can easily be done by using an ordinary combination square [3.10a], and by simply measuring in sequence from one cube to the next [3.10b]. It is helpful to draw lines representing the cross-sections on the cube assembly.

Once the cube locations are established for a given cross-section plane, they can be drawn on a pre-drawn grid sheet. There will be three sets of cross-sections, each set being either an x, y, or z set. Within each set, cross-sections will be taken at 1.5-inch (3.8 cm) intervals corresponding to the grid modules. Remember that each grid line represents an end view of a cross-section plane that is perpendicular to the plane upon which the grid is drawn. Each line on the pre-drawn grids will be labeled in correspondence to its location in the x,y,z coordinate system.

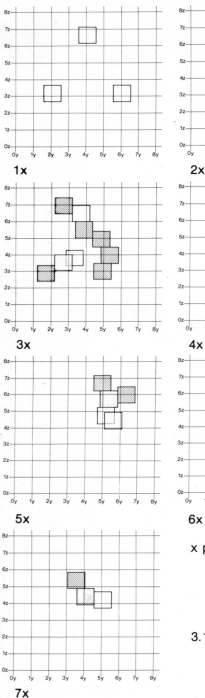

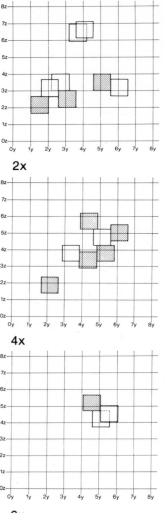

1x

2x

In the example shown in [3.11a–c], each set of cross-sections consists of seven planes. Note that diagonal lines are used to indicate cross-sections of the cubes, and that on occasion some of the cubes are not so indicated. This is because the cubes in question have their faces lying exactly on the plane of the cross-section. In some cases the cubes appear to overlap because they are positioned on either side of the plane of cross-section.

3x

4x

5x

6x

x planes

3.11a

7x

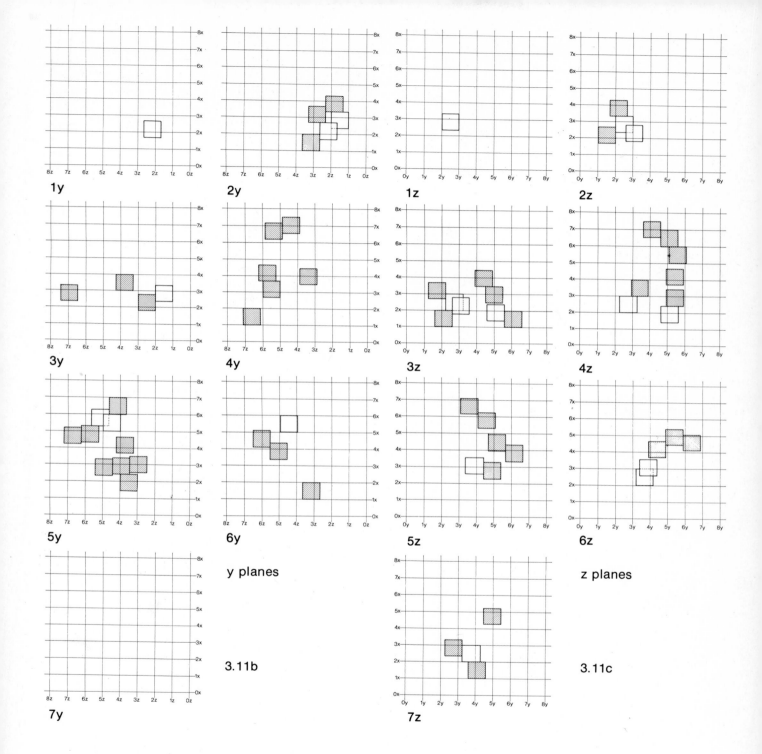

1y

2y

1z

2z

3y

4y

3z

4z

5y

6y

5z

6z

y planes

z planes

7y

3.11b

7z

3.11c

51

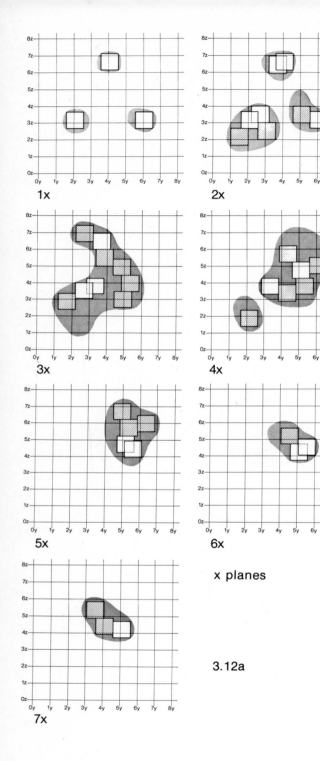

1x

2x

3x

4x

5x

6x

7x

x planes

3.12a

Once a complete set of sections for each of the x, y, and z planes is completed, the development of the contours may be started. The first step is to draw proposed contours that correspond to each cross-section [3.12a–c]. This must be done with great care since the contours will be the basis of the three-dimensional minimum-maximum envelope.

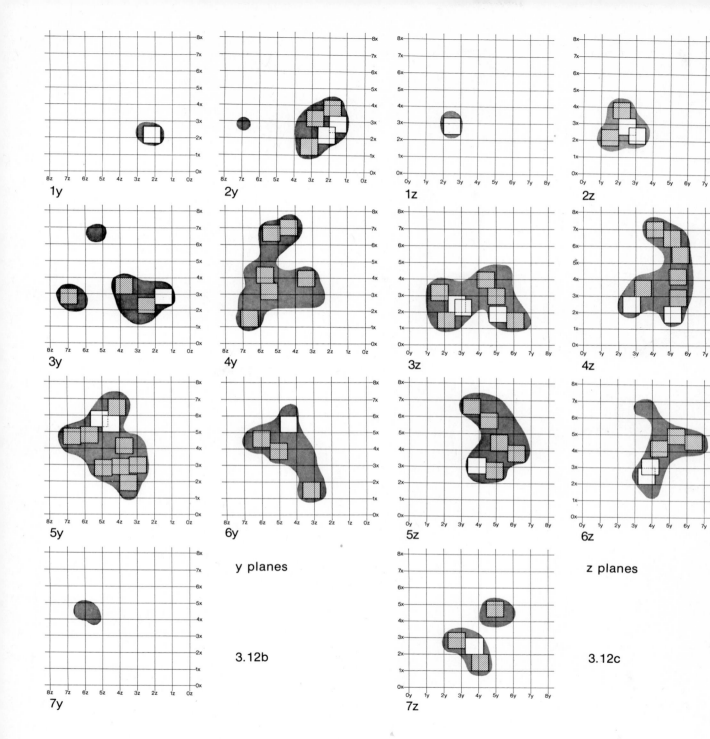

1y

2y

1z

2z

3y

4y

3z

4z

5y

6y

5z

6z

7y

y planes

3.12b

7z

z planes

3.12c

53

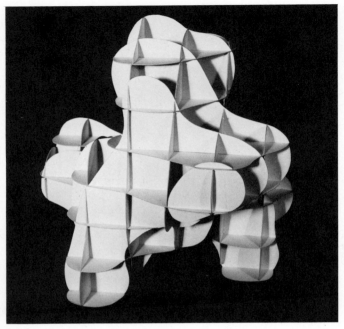

3.13a

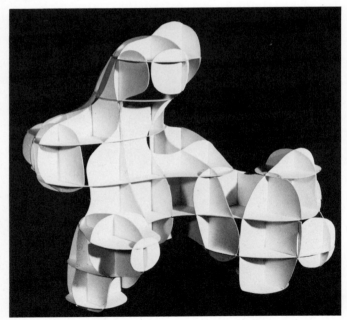

3.13b

The contour sections are incorporated into an egg crate model [3.13a–b] upon which the homogeneous minimum-maximum envelope will be fashioned. In the egg crate model, the contour sections are seen to intersect and thus create a clear volumetric visualization of the final envelope. Because these contours intersect, special attention must be given to insure that at the points on the outer surface where such intersections occur, the contours match exactly.

When a contour is drawn on a particular cross-section plane, it will of necessity cross many grid lines along its way. As we pointed out above, every grid line is an end view of another section plane. The point where the contour crosses such a grid line is a point that will be shared with a contour line on another cross-section, which is perpendicular to the plane of the contour line being drawn.

This requires the coordination of all the points of intersection generated by the contour lines. Such coordination is accomplished by a continual working back and forth from one section plane to another. Each time a contour line intersects a new grid line on its cross-section plane, another perpendicular plane is implicated. This particular part of the problem is perhaps the most difficult. It requires great accuracy, concentration, and attention to detail. If it is done well, however, the results will be satisfying.

The actual contour lines that are drawn are, at best, rough approximations no matter how accurately they are done. This is primarily because it is very difficult to visualize a three-dimensional structure on a two-dimensional plane. The contour lines as drawn should follow a meandering course, which generally corresponds to a form suggested by the cross-sections of the cubes and which is as gentle or gradual as possible. Changes in direction are to be distributed over the greatest distance. When the variation in curvature is so minimized, the principle of continuity is thus satisfied.

Since there is no way within the scope of this book to develop such curves with mathematical rigor, it is necessary to develop a keen intuitive sense of appropriateness with respect to such contours. This is not to say that one is left only with arbitrary decisions—in fact, quite the opposite is true.

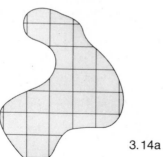

3.14a

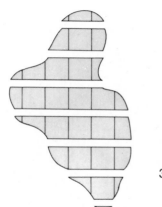

3.14b

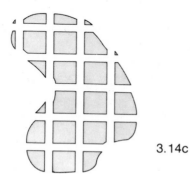

3.14c

The most elusive aspect of developing the contours is not how close to follow the cube sections, but how far away to stay. In the sections shown, there are certain parts of the curves that appear almost to touch the corners of the cubes, and others that are far away from the cubes. The former occur when the cubes in question fall on the section plane—the cubes without diagonal section lines. This is where it can be anticipated that the surface of the envelope will pass very close to the corners of such cubes.

When the contour lines appear to be far away from the cubes, the section is taken near the central regions of the cube, away from its corners. Also, the cross-sections on either side of a particular plane will have a fundamental determining role in the development of an appropriate contour for a given plane. Depending on where the cubes fall on adjacent cross-section planes, the contour line can move either further from or closer to the cubes on its own cross-sectional plane.

Once the complete set of cross-sectional contours are satisfactorily completed, the egg crate model can be constructed. This is accomplished by first transferring the contour drawing with grid from its cross-section plane to railroad board or other light-weight paper board. Use carbon paper to transfer the contour drawing.

Label each contour plane and each strip or segment with its respective number and coordinate planes. It is also useful to label the grid lines on each contour plane as well.

When this is finished, carefully cut out the complete set of x, y, and z contour planes. Leave the x planes intact [3.14a]. Cut the y planes into horizontal strips along the grid lines [3.14b]. Finally, cut the z planes into segments bounded by all horizontal and vertical grid lines [3.14c].

Note that the grid lines do not account for the thickness of the railroad board. Because of this, extra material corresponding to the thickness of the board should be removed along the grid lines. If this is not done, some annoying dimensional disparities in the finished model will occur.

3.15a

3.15b

These various components may now be assembled with glue into the appropriate number of x plane horizontal layers [3.15a]. Each layer may then be stacked to reveal the completed egg crate model [3.15b–e]. However, do not glue these stacked layers together at this point.

3.15c

3.15d

3.15e

3.16a

3.16b

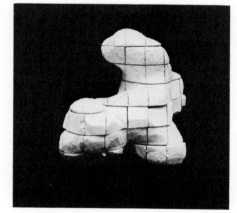

3.16c

With the egg crate layers completed, we are ready to begin the construction of the envelope form. Fill all the voids in the egg crate modules that are adjacent to the outer layer of surface of the envelope [3.16a]. The material to use for this purpose is rigid plastic foam—urethane or polystyrene. It should be roughly cut to fit the space and glued in place with white glue. Once all appropriate voids are filled, the entire assembly may be glued together [3.16b–c]. At this point the shape of the envelope becomes explicit.

In successive relatively thin layers, begin applying premixed Spackle or patching plaster to the assembly. Sanding between layers as necessary, begin perfecting the form and filling in all the gaps around the rigid foam. At this point, it will begin to become clear that the egg crate representation of the envelope needs to be improved.

It is unlikely that the three-dimensional reality of the minimum-maximum envelope can be fully anticipated in the two-dimensional grids. Typically, if the contours delineated by the egg crate model are strictly adhered to, the resulting envelope will exhibit a surface that is too acutely angular. Indeed, it will tend to have more surface area than is necessary and the continuity of its form will most likely require improvement. Nonetheless, the egg crate model provides for a very accurate point of departure and defines the limits of proximity for the envelope surface relative to the original random assembly of cubes.

When the envelope form is roughed out in conformation to the egg crate underpinnings, it becomes dramatically easier to critically assess the form's efficiency in satisfying the two objectives of minimum surface area and maximum distribution of stress. Look at each region in the form where the surfaces are doubly curved. If material is added, is the surface area likely to be reduced or increased? Usually this is relatively easy to judge by visual inspection.

Ask a similar question about the continuity of the form. Ask such questions over and over again. As material is added, layer by layer, sanded and resanded, and as the form is purged of its flaws, a point in the solution will be reached when the form will simply begin to look right. The surface area will approach its minimum, and the continuity of the form will be such that variation in curvature is minimized and stress is optimally distributed.

In comparing the final form with the egg crate model [3.17a–f], the gentler curves and greater coherence of the envelope's surface is revealed. It is almost always true that at the evolutionary point where the surface area is minimized and the distribution of stress is maximized, the form will take on a quality of rightness that is easily perceived. Envelope forms on either side of this evolutionary point will be markedly differentiated to those who pay attention to the inherent beauty of perfect form. Nature would not have it any other way.

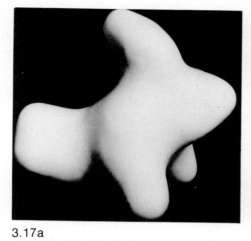

3.17a

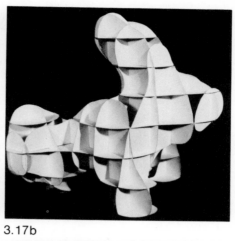

3.17b

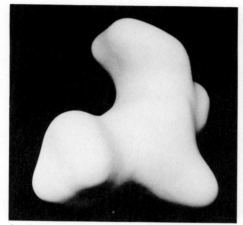

3.17c

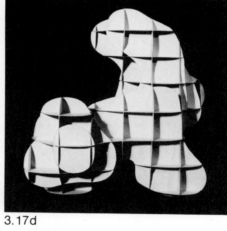

3.17d

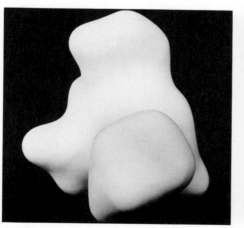

3.17e

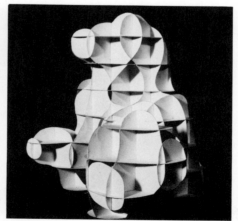

3.17f

Chapter 4:
The Synthesis of a Form

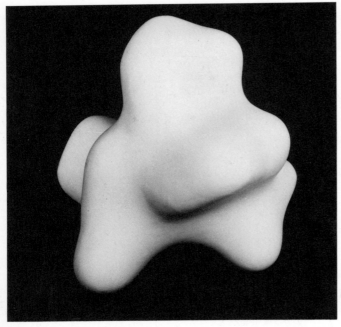

4.1a

4.1b

Problem 1: Polyhedral Approximation of the Minimum-Maximum Envelope

Problem

Using a network of triangular polygons, develop and construct a polyhedron which maps the contour of the minimum-maximum envelope built in Problem 2, Chapter 3. Select an average polygon size that is as large as possible but that is still able to provide for a convincing approximation of the overall form of the envelope [4.1a-b].

Extrinsic Forces

Configuration of the minimum-maximum envelope.

Intrinsic Forces

The inherent geometric constraints of three-dimensional space — particularly the properties of polyhedra and doubly curved surfaces.

Conceptual Guidelines

In the real world of built form, it is usually not possible to actually construct homogeneous structures, other than monoliths. Most structures are comprised of combinations of discrete elements. Such elements, for the most part, are geometrically quite simple and typically consist of flat surfaces or linear components.

If the construction of a complex form of the type represented by the contours of the minimum-maximum envelope were contemplated in the real world, a synthetic structure of some kind would no doubt be required. One such approach to synthesizing a form deals directly with the structure of the envelope's surface as an enclosure system.

4.2

The basic principles of space enclosing systems are found in the properties of polyhedra. A polyhedron is formed by enclosing a portion of three-dimensional space with four or more plane polygons [4.2]. A polygon is a portion of a plane bounded by three or more lines or segments. See Pearce and Pearce: *Polyhedra Primer* for an elementary presentation on polyhedra and related subjects. Some familiarity with the properties of polyhedra would be helpful in understanding the development of this problem.

It is usual that a polyhedron is derived as an assembly of unit polygons. The present problem proposes to derive a polyhedron as a "map" of an existing form. This mapping deviates from the formation of a classical polyhedron, whose shape is usually determined by the combination of sets of polygons of predetermined shapes. Certain polyhedra, however, can also be derived as polygonal maps of a sphere [4.3a-b].

Such spherical maps demonstrate that the corners, or vertices, of the polyhedra to which they are matched all fall on the surface of a common imaginary sphere. Therein lies the clue to the derivation of a polygonal map in the minimum-maximum envelope's surface. Specifically, a network of triangles will be derived by connecting points that lie on the surface of the minimum-maximum envelope.

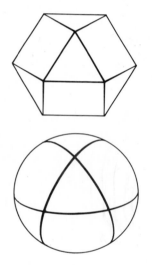

4.3a

4.3b

There are two important reasons why the polyhedron that maps the envelope's surface is derived using three-sided polygons (triangles). One is geometric and the other structural, and both reasons stem from the fact that the triangle is the only stable geometry in nature. The mathematics of trigonometry depends on triangulation, because the angles of a triangle are fixed by the lengths of its sides. Any geometric construction that is done without angular measurement can be done only as a combination of triangles. (See Pearce and Pearce: *Polyhedra Primer,* Chapter 7.) Indeed, such triangulated geometric constructions can be done entirely with compass and straight-edge.

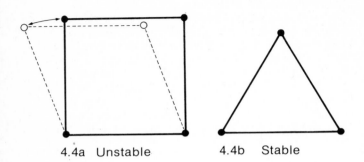

4.4a Unstable   4.4b Stable

Nontriangulated systems are unstable geometrically and structurally [4.4a]. Triangulated systems are the only ones that are inherently stable [4.4b]. Because of this, triangulated systems make the most efficient load-supporting structures. This was discussed briefly in Problem 3, Chapter 2, and it can be easily demonstrated by a simple experiment.

It is possible to construct two entirely different structures, each with twelve of the same kind of struts of common length, cross-sectional area, and material. One structure is the cube with 6 square faces [4.5a], and the other is the octahedron with 8 equilateral triangle faces [4.5b]. If each of these structures is loaded, with lead shot in this case, until it collapses, it is found that the octahedron performs 100 percent better than the cube [4.5c-f]. The cube collapses under almost exactly half the load, which is required to collapse the octahedron. In other words, for the same investment in resources, the octahedron does twice the work. For a more detailed discussion of this experiment see Pearce: *Structure in Nature Is a Strategy for Design*.

As we will see momentarily, the derivation of a polyhedron from a contoured envelope with polygons of more than three sides would be virtually impossible. There is no practical or efficient way to provide structural integrity for such an unsymmetrical form without the use of some form of triangulation.

4.5a

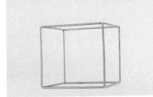

4.5b

4.5c

4.5d

4.5e

4.5f

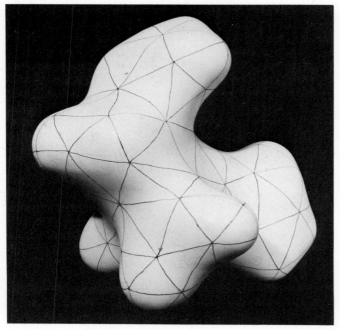

4.6

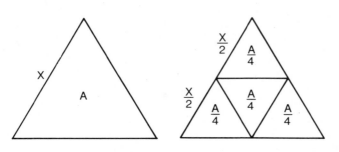

4.7

Techniques and Materials

Medium-weight or construction-weight paper is recommended for the construction of the polyhedral approximation of the minimum-maximum envelope. An ideal material is white cover stock or a 3-ply bristol board. The model will be assembled from polygons that are cut out of this board and taped together. Recommended tape is Scotch Brand Magic Tape, No. 810, ½ inch. Tools required include an X-Acto knife with a #11 blade, a metal straight-edge, and a cutting surface.

As a first step, lay out a proposed triangulated map directly on the surface of the finished minimum-maximum envelope [4.6]. This should be done free-hand with a pencil. An eraser can easily be used to make changes as you work. No drafting instruments need be used at this stage. After the final layout, as a rough free-hand configuration, has been settled on, establish the exact location of all of the vertices or corners where the triangles meet. This can be done by marking each with a precise ink dot.

Though the free-hand map is somewhat arbitrary, the relative size of the triangles used should be chosen carefully. Because the edges of the polygons will be straight lines, they will lie above or below the surface of the envelope. Only the vertices to which the edges of the triangles are connected lie on the surface of the envelope. It follows from this, that the smaller the edge lengths, the closer the mapping of triangles will conform to the actual surface of the envelope. Theoretically, with infinitely small triangles, the mapping would conform exactly to the surface of the envelope.

Remember, however, that when a possible average edge length is half the length of another possible average edge length, the number of polygons generated to map the surface will be increased by a factor of four [4.7]. Therefore, there is an incentive to make the relative size of the average polygon edge to be as large as possible in order to minimize the number of triangular faces. The polyhedral approximation shown in [4.1b] has 148 faces.

Tetrahedron (4-hedron)   Triangular Dipyramid (6-hedron)

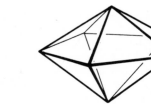

Octahedron (8-hedron)   Pentagonal Dipyramid (10-hedron)

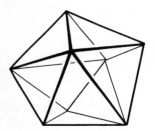

12-hedron   14-hedron

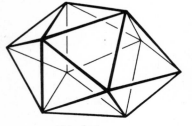

16-hedron   Icosahedron (20-hedron)

4.8

The goal is to develop a mapping layout which consists of the largest possible triangles that will still convincingly represent the overall shape of the minimum-maximum envelope form. The recommended edge length range is from 1½ to 2½ inches (3.8 to 6.4 cm). Consistent with the criterion of maximum distribution of stress, the variation of edge length should be minimized. That is, the sides of the triangles which comprise the mapping of the envelope surface should be as close in length to each other as possible.

Note that it is impossible to construct a mapping of the envelope's surface with equilateral triangles — triangles whose sides are equal. The inherent properties of space prevent this. Since the interior angle of the equilateral triangle is always 60°, there are only a small number of ways these polygons can be combined around a single vertex.

If we were mapping the sphere with equilateral triangles, there are only three possible configurations: the regular tetrahedron, the regular octahedron, and the regular icosahedron. In addition to these three regular polyhedra, there are five more that form the family of all possible convex polyhedra assembled from equilateral triangles. These eight polyhedra are known as the deltahedra [4.8].

Note the number of triangles meeting at a single vertex. Only three variations are exhibited — three, four, or five triangles meeting at a vertex. If six equilateral triangles were to meet at a single vertex, the sum of their angles would equal 360°. This would cause all six triangles to lie on a flat plane thereby preventing any convexity to occur. Without this convexity, closure is impossible and without closure, polyhedra cannot be formed.

In order to map the surface of the minimum-maximum envelope with triangles, variations of interior angles must be allowed. However, since the goal is to lay out the triangles so that their differences in edge length are minimized, it is useful to have in mind approximations of equilateral triangles.

Once the triangular mapping is finalized, number the triangles, and make sure each vertex is precisely indicated with an ink dot. You will now proceed to lay out a network of triangles in a logical sequence on the bristol board [4.9]. It is usually easier to construct a polyhedron model by drawing a network and folding the faces to meet one another, rather than cutting each face out individually and taping them together.

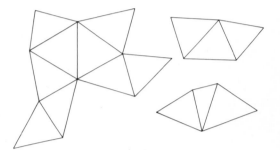

4.9

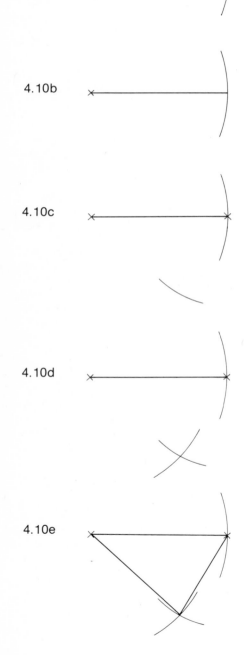

4.10a

4.10b

4.10c

4.10d

4.10e

Begin the network by choosing an arbitrary triangle that falls in a convex region of the minimum-maximum envelope. Using a compass, place the pivot point on a vertex of the triangle. Adjust the compass so that the drawing point matches a vertex immediately next to the original vertex. Lift the compass off the envelope, and on the board you are using for the network, draw a short arc segment [4.10a]. Draw a straight line that connects the pivot point of the compass with the arc segment [4.10b]. The point where the straight line joins the arc is now a new pivot point that corresponds to the neighboring vertex.

Place the compass back on the surface of the envelope at this neighboring vertex. Spread the compass the length of the second edge of the triangle. Return the compass to the board and swing an arc from the second vertex [4.10c]. Place the compass on the envelope, this time on the first pivot point or vertex. Spread the compass the length of the third side. Once again return the compass to the board, with the pivot point at the first vertex. Swing the arc, which is the length of the third side, to intersect with the other arc [4.10d]. Draw straight lines to connect this vertex to the first two [4.10e]. At this moment, the first triangle of the network has been drawn.

Repeat this procedure, drawing each successive triangle one by one. Number each triangle on the board as you go. Make sure to keep track, triangle by triangle, of orientation and of common edges and vertices. Draw the lines with a relatively hard and very sharp pencil. Accuracy is of the utmost importance to assure proper fitting of all polygons during assembly. It is easy to get lost in this procedure, so pay careful attention.

As you progress, you will discover that it is impossible to lay out a network which includes the entire polyhedron in one mapping. It will require at least two networks, and more likely, three or four with a few left over isolated polygons. This is because the polyhedron of the envelope has both convex and concave regions. An ordinary well-behaved convex polyhedron can be laid out in one continuous network. The layout was begun with an arbitrary triangle that falls in a convex region of the envelope. As the network progresses, however, there will often be choices about the placement of successive triangles, because the triangles that share two of its sides may already be in the network. The position chosen is a matter of layout efficiency having no effect on the final result.

With the layout completed, cutting, scoring, and folding can begin. Cut out the perimeter of the network with an X-Acto knife and metal straight-edge. Make sure that the blade remains parallel to the edge of the straight-edge as you are cutting. Hold the straight-edge firmly so it will not slip since it serves as a guide for the cutting line. Using slight pressure against the straight-edge, cut each outside edge of the network with several sure strokes of moderate pressure until the edge is cut completely through. Always cut on a cutting surface, such as heavy chipboard, to avoid cutting table surfaces and to prolong the life of the knife blade.

After each piece of the network is cut out, the triangle edges that are shared with adjacent triangles must be scored for folding. Scoring can be done with an X-Acto knife or a pointed, blunt instrument such as a ballpoint pen. This choice depends on what kind of board you are scoring. Experimentation is useful to determine the best tool.

Using the straight-edge, score along the lines between adjacent triangles. Remember that you are creating a score or crease to facilitate a clean fold of the somewhat stiff board. Once again, score along the edges with great accuracy. By comparing the numbers on the triangles in the network with those on the subdivided surface of the envelope, it is possible to tell in advance whether a given edge is going to be convex or concave. The best looking model usually results from scoring all lines on the outside of the surface. If a knife is used, however, the concave lines should also be scored on the inside.

Once cutting and scoring is completed, the network layouts are ready to be folded and assembled. Fold the scored edges in the proper direction to resemble the minimum-maximum envelope. Tape is used to join adjacent triangles that are separate and not folded. Join the common edges by cutting off a piece of tape slightly longer than the edge to be joined. Lay half of one side of the tape along the edge of one of the triangles. Bring the next triangle into position under the other half of the tape and join the two adjacent polygons [4.11]. Using a blunt tool, burnish the tape. Cut off the extra lengths of tape.

Continue to fold and tape and assemble the polyhedron in a logical sequence. You will probably end up with two large sections to be joined as a last step. This will require some care and a bit of finesse.

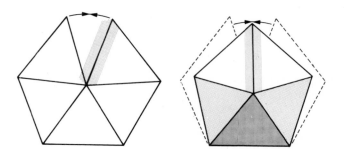

4.11

Compare the final assembled polyhedron to the minimum-maximum envelope form [4.12a-b]. Do you have a convincing approximation? The resulting polyhedron provides a structural representation of the minimum-maximum envelope. Like the original form, it has the same tendency to minimize surface area and to maximize distribution of stress. It accomplishes this synthesis, however, as an assembly of components, which have great advantages for construction logistics. It demonstrates a strategy that enables unsymmetrical three-dimensional envelopes to be constructed from component parts.

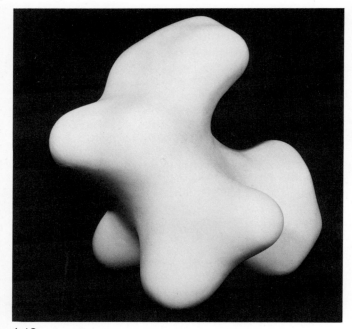

4.12a

4.12b

Problem 2: Structural Framework Approximation of the Minimum-Maximum Envelope

Problem
Construct a structural framework which has the properties of local and global stability and is based upon the network of the polygonal map of Problem 1, Chapter 4. Strut lenghts used to assemble the framework must be twice the length of their corresponding edges in the triangulated polyhedron.

Extrinsic Forces
Configuration of the triangulated polyhedron that is the approximation of the minimum-maximum envelope.

Intrinsic Forces
The inherent properties of geometric structures and the conditions that govern inherent stability.

Conceptual Guidelines
Having completed the polyhedron that approximates the minimum-maximum envelope, notice its structural behavior. Although it will readily support its own weight, it exhibits some instability. If the paper polyhedron is placed on its three base points and pushed down upon, some flexibility can be observed as the structure deflects [4.13a-b]. It won't collapse entirely, but it may deflect quite markedly.

Although this polyhedron is entirely composed of triangles, the three-dimensional arrangement of these triangles is such that it is not completely stable. It exhibits overall or global stability, which prevents it from totally collapsing, but suffers from local instability, which allows it to deflect at certain points. This primarily results from the combination of convex and concave regions within the polyhedron. The regions where convex and concave areas meet, often exhibit a localized instability caused by the structural ambiguity of such transition points.

4.13a

4.13b

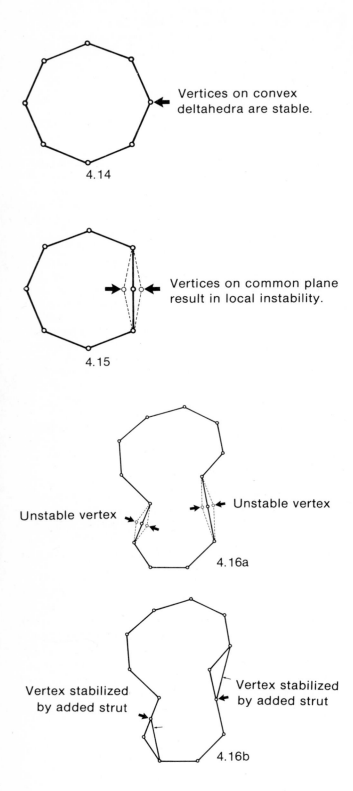

Vertices on convex deltahedra are stable.

4.14

Vertices on common plane result in local instability.

4.15

Unstable vertex

Unstable vertex

4.16a

Vertex stabilized by added strut

Vertex stabilized by added strut

4.16b

The deltadedra, which consist entirely of triangles and are convex [4.8], satisfy the requirements of both local and global stability, and are as a result completely rigid. If a framework of any of the convex deltrahedra is constructed with flexible joints, it will be completely rigid with its stability provided by its geometry [4.14].

If the framework of the convex-concave deltahedron of the minimum-maximum envelope is constructed with flexible joints, it will not be completely rigid. The question is how can it be made completely rigid? How can its stability be guaranteed by its geometry? That such a structure must be triangulated goes without saying, but apparently that is not quite enough.

A triangulated polyhedral framework will suffer from local instability when many, if not all, the triangles surrounding any given vertex share a common plane, or nearly share a common plane [4.15]. When such a condition occurs, stability is not fully three-dimensional as the triangulation is, in effect, only two-dimensional. Some limited motion can usually occur perpendicular to the shared plane. If it occurs frequently enough in the wrong places, this local instability can lead to significant apparent global instability and hence large overall deflections. This phenomenon often occurs with the triangulated frameworks of polyhedra which incorporate both convex and concave regions.

We can say then, that local instability results when the triangulated framework provides for two-dimensional stability only. It follows from this that the elimination of local instability in a system is to provide the missing three-dimensional stability. In order to do this, the position of an unstable vertex needs to be fixed in all directions. This can be accomplished by adding additional strategically placed struts to the original framework. Such struts can be added to the inside or outside of the envelope of the original framework. They will typically connect neighboring pairs of vertices which appear to have an unstable relationship to one another [4.16a-b]. The goal is to add no more struts than is necessary to insure that the geometry of the structure provides for the complete stability of the polyhedral framework.

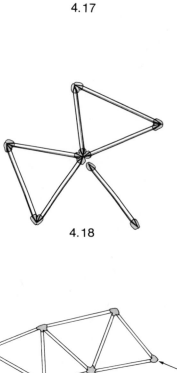

4.17

4.18

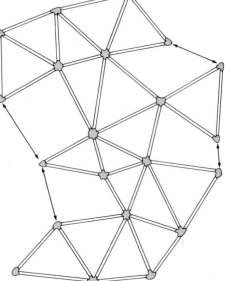

4.19

Techniques and Materials

Various materials and techniques can be used to develop this structural model. Round wooden dowels, ⅛-inch (3 mm) in diameter, will work as well as anything. Since accuracy is crucial, it is helpful to taper the ends of the dowels to minimize the detrimental dimensional effects of the dowels' thickness. This is easily done with a pencil sharpener, especially if it is electrically powered [4.17].

Since the framework must be held together with hingeable connectors, we recommend making connections with Barge Cement. This is a highly flexible, rubbery cement that is easy to use. Just dip the ends of precut dowels in the cement, let set for a few seconds, and then join together [4.18].

Another way to use the Barge Cement is to tape the struts down to a flat surface in the form of the original network map, put a blob of cement at each vertex, and let dry [4.19]. Cover your work area with a sheet of polyethylene or transparent food wrap. Cement or glue will not stick to polyethylene and thus your working surface can remain clean. After the cement is thoroughly dry, the network can be folded into its proper three-dimensional configuration with the necessary additional connections made as required. Carefully done, the Barge Cement method will produce a good, strong permanent model which will demonstrate, because of its flexibility, the local instability of the original structure and then the complete stability of the modified triangulated framework.

The strut components are to be cut twice as long as their corresponding edges in the original triangulated polyhedron. Careful planning will be required if confusion is to be avoided. Once the basic double-size framework is completed, it can be evaluated with respect to its stability.

Place the completed polyhedron framework on a flat surface. Push on it at various vertices. Notice where deflection occurs. Continue to push on every vertex within the structure. Try to observe empirically where instabilities exhibit themselves. Consider the most efficient locations for additional struts, which will add to the stability. Begin adding struts. Remember that new strut locations can always be changed if they don't prove to be effective.

As struts are added, notice how stability improves. It should take very few additional struts to establish complete stability. Once this complete stability has been achieved, it can be assumed that a structure of very high efficiency relative to the original minimum-maximum envelope has been constructed. The high strength-to-weight characteristics of a fully three-dimensional triangulated polyhedron that has been properly designed can be readily appreciated. Direct experience with the structural framework approximation of the minimum-maximum envelope will bring this to light.

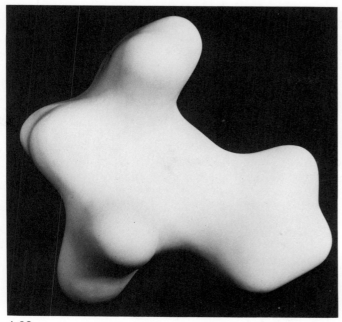

4.20a

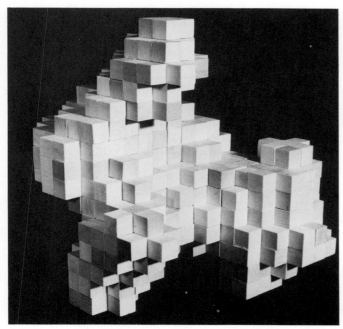

4.20b

Problem 3: Incremental Approximation of the Minimum-Maximum Envelope — Cubes

Problem
Assemble an incremental approximation of the minimum-maximum envelope with a space filling array of ¾-inch (1.9 cm) cubes [4.20a-b]. The cubes are to be packed with no space left over in such a way that faces of adjacent cubes exactly match. The form of the completed space filling assembly of cubes should exhibit a convincing approximation of the overall form of the minimum-maximum envelope.

Extrinsic Forces
Configuration of the minimum-maximum envelope.

Intrinsic Forces
Specific shape and symmetry properties of the cube, which govern the possible spatial arrangements of aggregates of cubes, and the properties of three-dimensional space in general, which govern all spatial arrangements of physical components.

Conceptual Guidelines
Earlier we looked at the question of building structures in the real world with the polyhedral approximation of the minimum-maximum envelope (Problem 1, Chapter 4). That particular approach dealt directly with the structure of the envelope by mapping with polygons which subdivided its surface. The mapping reduced the homogeneous surface of the envelope to an assembly of components. In the real world, it is virtually impossible to construct anything without the use of components. Another way to look at the need to use components for the construction of complex form is through volumetric incrementation — that is, by deriving a modular approximation by the subdivision of the volume enclosed by the minimum-maximum envelope, rather than as a subdivision of its surface.

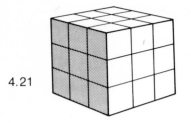

4.21

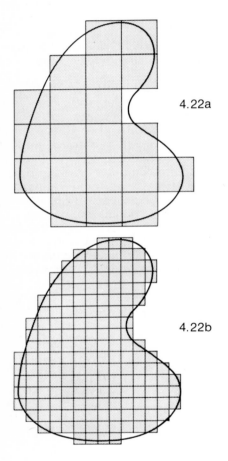

4.22a

4.22b

The classic and most commonly used system for the incremental or equal subdivision of space is the space filling of equal cubes. This geometry is also known as the Cartesian or x,y,z coordinate system, which we have already used in Problem 2, Chapter 3. It is also the system upon which most of our architecture is based, and it is a system familiar to most children of pre-school age.

Normally when cubes are packed to fill space, the tendency is to build larger cubes [4.21]. The overall shape of the space filling array is given by the shape of the space filling unit. The boundary conditions are prosaic. The problem here is to match as closely as possible the boundary of a space filling array of cubes with the overall shape of the minimum-maximum envelope.

The closeness of the match is a function of the size of the increment relative to the overall size of the form. The smaller the increment, the closer the match [4.22a-b]. On the other hand, when the relative size of the modular increment is reduced, the number of modules needed increases geometrically. If the linear dimension of the modular increment is reduced by half, the quantity of cubes required will increase by a factor of eight [4.23a-c]. Therefore, the dimension of the modular increment must be chosen with some consideration. We have suggested the ¾-inch (1.9 cm) cube as the largest modular increment that will still provide a reasonable approximation of the envelope. Obviously a ⅜-inch (9.5 mm) cube would provide a closer approximation, but since it would require 8 times as many cubes, it would take approximately 8 times as long to construct.

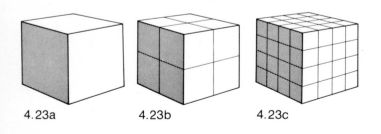

4.23a   4.23b   4.23c

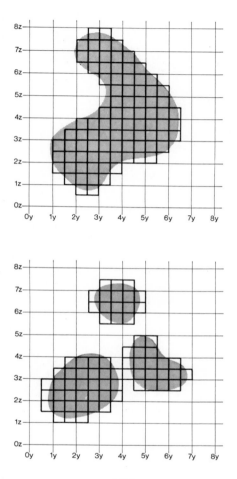

4.24

Techniques and Materials

The ¾-inch (1.9 cm) cubes can be fabricated from clear pine or other kinds of wood. Pine boards ¾-inch (1.9 cm) thick are available and can be readily cut into cubes with a table saw or radial arm saw. Since these boards, called "one by's," can vary in thickness, make sure that the square blocks you cut have edges that are equal to the actual measured thickness of the board. Make sure all the cubes to be used in the model are cut from boards of the same thickness. It is important that all cubes used will be of exactly the same dimensions. The number of ¾-inch cubes required will vary between 700 and 1000 depending on the configuration.

Once all the cubes are cut, the procedure for the construction of the space filling assembly is quite simple. First, lay out all of the horizontal section (x) planes that were prepared for the contour sections of the egg crate model [3.14]. Tape these drawings down to a flat surface and cover with a thin transparent film of polyethylene such as food wrap. Lay out a single layer of cubes on each of these section planes. The cubes should align with the 1½-inch (3.8 cm) grid of the section planes and should approximately follow the contour [4.24]. The example shows two out of seven planes. These planar arrays of cubes are then glued together with white glue. The food wrap protects the drawings from the glue.

After a planar array of cubes is preassembled for each horizontal section, they are assembled in layers to form a complete space filling approximation of the minimum-maximum envelope. However, since the original sections are on a 1½-inch (3.8 cm) grid, these layers of ¾-inch (1.9 cm) cubes must be spaced apart with intermediate layers of ¾-inch (1.9 cm) cubes. When joining a pair of preassembled layers of cubes, add the intermediate layer to the smaller of the two preassembled layers. When adding these additional cubes, use the glue sparingly so that incorrectly placed cubes may be removed. Pay careful attention to the vertical alignment of the layers as they are assembled into a complete structure. Also note that the layers are built on the top side of the original horizontal section drawings — an orientation that must be preserved as these layers are assembled to complete the space filling array.

As a final step, with all the layers glued together, compare the space filling array to the minimum-maximum envelope [4.25a-d]. It is highly likely that some additional cubes will need to be added to make a more convincing approximation of the envelope. This fine tuning can be done only by very careful spatial observation and decision. Once this incremental approximation of the envelope is completed, some of the limitations of the cubic geometry for the representation of complex spatial configurations can be appreciated. Although it is clear that the space filling model can approximate the minimum-maximum envelope, it is not an altogether satisfying approximation.

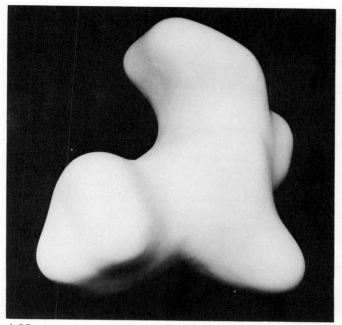

4.25a

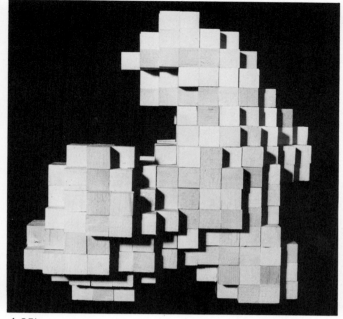

4.25b

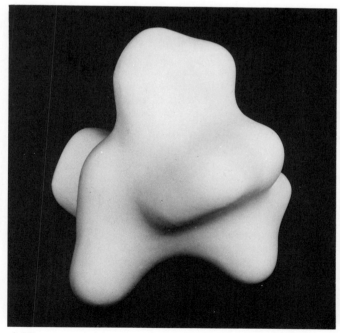

4.25c

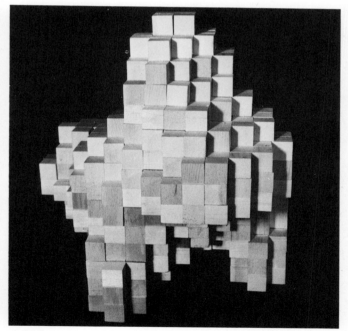

4.25d

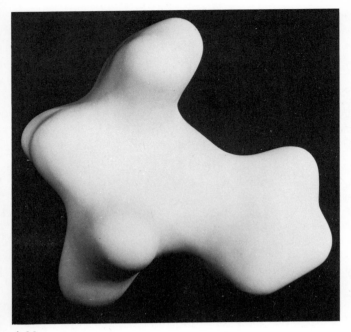

4.26a

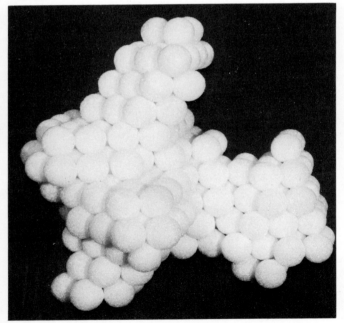

4.26b

Problem 4: Incremental Approximation of the Minimum-Maximum Envelope — Spheres

Problem
Assemble an incremental approximation of the minimum-maximum envelope with a closest packed array of equal spheres of 1¼-inch (3.2 cm) diameter [4.26a-b]. The spheres are to be assembled in correspondence with a 60° spatial grid derived from the closest packing of equal spheres. The overall form of the sphere packing assembly should match, as nearly as possible, the overall form of the minimum-maximum envelope.

Extrinsic Forces
Configuration of the minimum-maximum envelope

Intrinsic Forces
Specific shape and symmetry properties of the sphere, which govern the spatial arrangements of spheres in closest packed aggregates, and properties of three-dimensional space in general, which govern all spatial arrangements of physical components.

Conceptual Guidelines
The use of a closest packed array of equal spheres is another way to approach the problem of volumetric incrementation. A three-dimensional network can be derived by connecting with straight lines the centers of nearest neighbor spheres in a closest packed array. When this is done, a 60° spatial grid is generated in which twelve lines meet at every point within the grid. This grid is in marked contrast to the grid which is generated by the space filling of cubes as seen in Problem 3, Chapter 4. With the 90° system of the cubes, only 6 lines meet at every point within the grid.

The importance of considering the 60° grid, which is generated by closest packed spheres, is two-fold. First, it is more adaptive to variations of configuration by virtue of having more angular options than a 90° system. Second, it leads inherently to triangulated structures which, as we have already seen, offer substantial structural advantages.

4.27

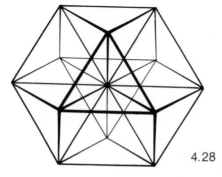

4.28

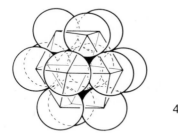

4.29

In a planar array of closest packed equal spheres, six spheres always surround a seventh. When sphere centers are connected, a regular hexagon comprised of six equilateral triangles is formed [4.27]. In a three-dimensional array of closest packed equal spheres, each sphere is exactly surrounded by twelve others. When the sphere centers are connected, four intersecting regular hexagons are formed comprised of 24 equilateral triangles meeting at a point in the center sphere. Twelve lines meeting at the sphere center are thus defined [4.28]. The twelve spheres surrounding the central sphere define the vertices of a polyhedron known as the cuboctahedron [4.29].

Sphere packing assemblies can be used to account for a variety of polyhedral shapes, a subject that is treated in depth in Pearce: *Structure in Nature Is a Strategy for Design.* It becomes apparent that a large range of shape and pattern can be accounted for with closest packed equal spheres.

As was the case with the space filling of cubes, the smaller the modular increment relative to the overall size of the minimum-maximum envelope, the closer will be the match in the final form. However, the smaller the increment, the larger the number of modules that will be required, by an 8-fold factor. There is an incentive, therefore, to have the modular increment as large as it can be while still enabling an acceptable approximation of the minimum-maximum envelope to be assembled. To this end, we have suggested the 1¼-inch (3.2 cm) diameter sphere.

As it turns out, when compared to the space filling of cubes, the sphere packing model shown here provides a more convincing level of approximation of the envelope. This is accomplished with only about 300 spheres of 1¼-inch (3.2 cm), whereas roughly 700 ¾-inch (3.2 cm) cubes were required for a satisfactory representation of the minimum-maximum envelope. This apparent superior efficiency of the sphere packing system stems primarily from its greater number of combinatorial options per modular increment.

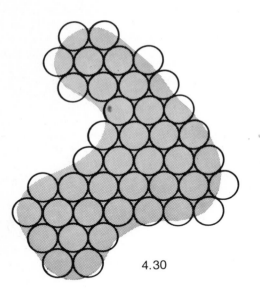

4.30

4.31

Techniques and Materials

Styrofoam plastic spheres are usually readily available in a variety of sizes. If 1¼-inch (3.2 cm) are not available, 1-inch (2.5 cm) will work as well. Equal sized spheres of other materials are also satisfactory as long as they can be glued together. There is probably no material, however, that is quite as convenient to work with or as inexpensive as the Styrofoam. Sphere assemblies should be glued with white glue or aliphatic resin glue, the latter being faster drying and thus easier to work with. Do not use solvent type glues, such as model cement, since the Styrofoam, which has poor chemical resistance, will dissolve before your eyes. Approximately 300 spheres will be needed.

Select an intermediate horizontal section from the set of x plane contours, which were prepared for the egg crate model. This contour should be one of the largest in the set of x planes. Tape this drawing to a flat surface and cover it with clear food wrap or polyethylene.

Lay out a planar array of spheres over this contour drawing [4.30]. Does it seem to be a good approximation? If not, try another orientation. Try to have rows of spheres align with one axis of the original grid. This helps maintain a frame of reference to earlier phases of this study. Remember that each sphere on this planar layer will be surrounded by six others except at the boundary. Note that spheres will align in three sets of axes, parallel to the sides of an equilateral triangle [4.31].

Once you have arrived at a satisfactory configuration for this first planar array of spheres, carefully glue them together. Do not disturb or lose track of the configuration. Use glue sparingly with a drop located at the tangent point where one sphere touches another.

With the first planar array of spheres glued together, successive layers of spheres are added first to one side, then to the other. It is recommended that most of, if not all, the spheres be added entirely to one side of the first layers, prior to adding any to the other side. When spheres are added to the first layer, they will naturally want to be placed in the low spots, which are vertically above the space between spheres in the layer underneath. Each new sphere will rest on three spheres in the layer below.

4.32

Notice that only every other low spot or space on the layer below can be occupied by the newly added spheres. Choose the set of low spots that seems to provide for the most useful position for the added-on spheres. Once this choice is made for a second layer, the spheres in every third layer must be positioned vertically above the spaces of the first layer that are not covered by the second layer [4.32]. If this is not done, a less symmetrical or even random arrangement of closest packed spheres will result. This would disrupt the planer continuity of equilateral triangles and can be a source of disorientation. Continue to add the spheres in an orderly sequence to keep from getting lost and to preserve a consistent orientation of the sphere packing form to the minimum-maximum envelope.

The process of adding spheres relies on good judgement through extremely careful observation in attempting to match the evolving sphere packing assembly to the original minimum-maximum envelope. As the sphere packing assembly evolves, you will see that it is an effective incremental approximation of the minimum-maximum envelope [4.33a-d]. Although it is less familiar than the cubic system, the geometric attributes of the sphere packing suggest that it deserves attention as a spatial vocabulary. The problems that follow explore some of these attributes further.

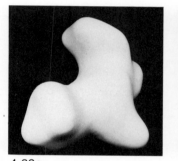

4.33a

4.33b

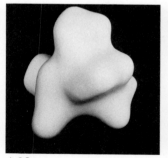

4.33c

4.33d

Problem 5: Polyhedral Envelope Derived from Sphere Packing Approximation of the Minimum-Maximum Envelope

4.34a

4.34b

4.35a

4.35b

Problem

Develop and construct a polyhedron envelope, which corresponds to the outer layer of spheres in the sphere packing approximation of the minimum-maximum envelope [4.34a-b]. (See Problem 4, Chapter 5.) The faces of this polyhedron are to be derived by joining the centers of the successive neighboring spheres. The sphere centers are the vertices of polygons and the connections between the sphere centers are the edges of the polygons. This polyhedron is to match exactly the overall shape of the sphere packing from which it is derived. It should also roughly approximate the overall form of the minimum-maximum envelope from which the sphere packing was derived [4.35a-b].

Extrinsic Forces

Configuration of the sphere packing approximation of the minimum-maximum envelope.

Intrinsic Forces

The 60° spatial grid defined by the closest packed spheres, and the possible subdivisions of that grid.

Conceptual Guidelines

In Problem 1, Chapter 4 we developed the concept of a polyhedron approximation of the minimum-maximum envelope. In that instance, a synthetic structure was created by mapping polygons on the surface of the envelope. We then looked at two incremental approaches to the problem of synthesizing a structure that corresponds to the overall shape of the envelope. One of these incremental structures was created by means of an assembly of closest packed spheres.

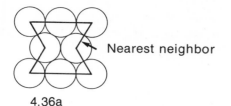

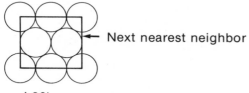

Nearest neighbor

4.36a

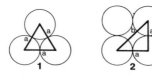

Next nearest neighbor

4.36b

In this new structure, by considering the boundary layer of spheres as vertices, it is possible to synthesize another polyhedron that corresponds to the minimum-maximum envelope. Since the polyhedron in this case, however, is derived through the intermediary of the sphere packing, it does not match the original envelope form as closely as does the polyhedron which maps the contour of the original form. Indeed, the polyhedron which is derived from the sphere packing is governed by a unique set of geometric relationships given by that assembly of volumetric modular increments.

A polyhedron consisting of a curious collection of polygons can be easily derived from the sphere packing. The polyhedron must have all of its vertices at the centers of spheres on the outer or boundary layer of the closest packed assembly. Polygons are generated by connecting these vertices at sphere centers with straight line segments. Vertices may be connected which are at the centers of nearest neighbor or next nearest neighbor spheres [4.36a-b].

A set of six basic triangles can be generated from combinations of nearest and next nearest neighbor connections [4.37]. Triangle #1 is the basic equilateral triangle with an edge length equal to the 1¼-inch (3.2 cm) diameter of the spheres from which it is derived. Note that all six triangles are constructed with combinations of three edge lengths — a,b, and c — and that all three edge lengths are generated by the first three triangles 1, 2, and 3.

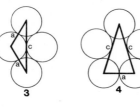

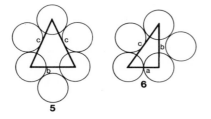

4.37

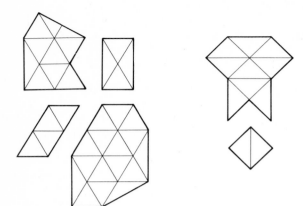

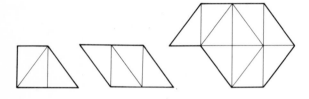

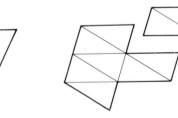

The boundary layer in the sphere packing model defines a collection of plane polygons — each of which is one of these six triangles or a multiple of one of these six. Some typical examples of multiple polygons are shown in [4.38].

Techniques and Materials

The materials, tools, and construction techniques for modeling this polyhedron are essentially the same as those used in Problem 1, Chapter 4. Only the derivation of the polyhedron is completely different.

Look carefully at the sphere packing model. Identify the most appropriate combination of polygons keeping the overall form of the minimum-maximum envelope in mind at all times. Make a set of paperboard templates of the six basic triangles and perhaps some of the basic quadrilaterals shown in [4.38]. Use these templates to lay out the larger polygons directly on to the paperboard from which they will be cut out. These polygons can either be drawn individually or as a partial network for the polyhedron. On each large polygon, indicate lightly in pencil the layout of basic triangles which comprise the larger polygon. Each polygonal plane should be laid out and cut out in a single piece.

With the polygons or networks of polygons cut out, proceed to assemble the polyhedron using the taping technique described in Problem 1, Chapter 4. Once again, remember the need for accuracy at all stages of construction.

4.38

Once this polyhedron is completed, it is interesting to compare it to the triangulated polyhedron of Problem 1 and to compare both polyhedra to the minimum-maximum envelope [4.39a-c]. Although the polyhedron derived from the sphere packing does not match the minimum-maximum envelope nearly as closely as does the triangulated polyhedron approximation, it does show a good relationship in overall form. The sphere packing polyhedron is definitely a compromise, but a useful one when consideration is given to the fact that it is generated from only six different kinds of triangular polygons. Remember that the triangulated polyhedron, which so elegantly maps the contour of the minimum-maximum envelope, requires 148 different triangles with none used more than once. In these polyhedral approximations of the envelope, one approach favors component simplification, and the other favors a literal response to the extrinsic forces given by the form. Both approaches are valid — the priorities are different.

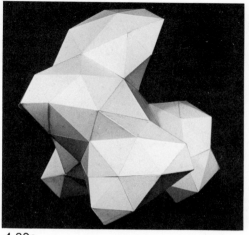

4.39a

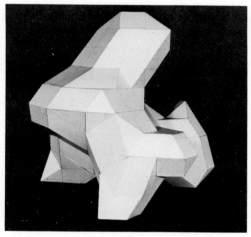

4.39b

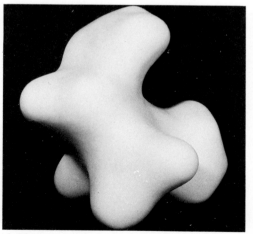

4.39c

Problem 6: Framework Structure Supporting Horizontal Planes Derived from Sphere Packing Approximation of the Minimum-Maximum Envelope

Problem

Develop and construct a stable framework structure, which supports a series of horizontal planes, based upon the sphere packing approximation of the minimum-maximum envelope [4.40a-b]. The framework should correspond to the outer layer of spheres in the packing and should, therefore, exactly match the polyhedron envelope from Problem 6 [4.41a-b]. The horizontal planes should coincide with each layer of spheres in the packing. Like the polyhedron envelope from which it is derived, this framework will also roughly approximate the overall form of the envelope [4.42a-b].

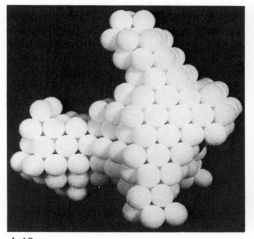

4.40a

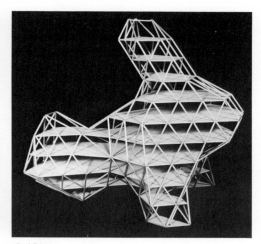

4.40b

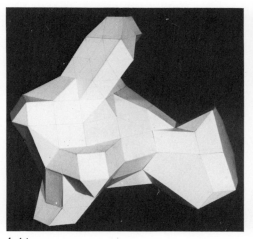

4.41a

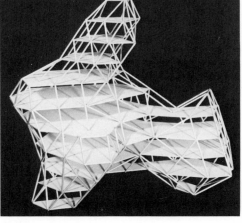

4.41b

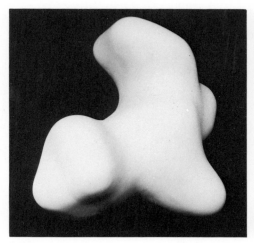

4.42a

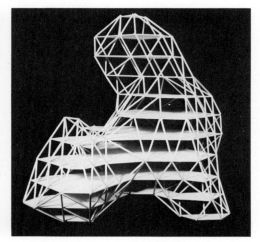

4.42b

Extrinsic Forces
Configuration of the sphere packing approximation of the minimum-maximum envelope.

Intrinsic Forces
The 60° grid defined by the closest packed spheres, and the possible subdivisions of that grid.

Conceptual Guidelines
Since the polyhedron envelope that corresponds to the sphere packing is generated from a series of six basic triangles, the prospects for constructing a corresponding stable framework structure would seem to be quite good. We know that the condition of stability will require a triangulated framework. Therefore, all that would seem to be necessary is the construction of a framework whose struts match the edges of the triangles that comprise the faces of the polyhedron, which is derived from the sphere packing. Indeed, this is exactly the case. In many instances, however, the faces of the polyhedron are composed of planar arrays of triangles. We have seen before that such a condition will give rise to local instabilities. Since it is given that this framework must support a series of horizontal planes, we can look to these very planes to prevent local instabilities.

Techniques and Materials
The materials, tools, and construction techniques required for this framework structure are the familiar ones we have used earlier, with some variations. The horizontal planes need to be cut from mat or illustration board of approximately 1/16-inch (1.6 mm) thickness. The struts ideally should be 1/16-inch (1.6 mm) diameter wood dowels. Swab sticks or round toothpicks are about right, although bass wood or balsa wood square sticks may be used if round sticks are not available. The best glue to use for this problem is Testors cement for wood models.

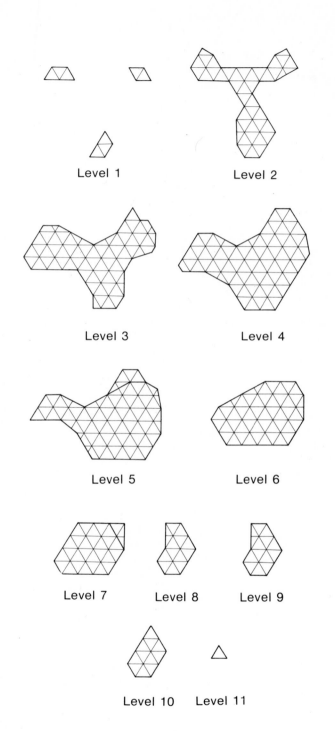

Level 1　　　　　　Level 2

Level 3　　　　　　Level 4

Level 5　　　　　　Level 6

Level 7　　Level 8　　Level 9

Level 10　Level 11

4.43

In developing the configuration for each horizontal plane, it is best to first consider the polyhedron envelope derived from the sphere packing. Notice that these horizontal planes will intersect the polyhedron envelope on lines that already exist. These lines are the edges of the polygons from which the polyhedron is assembled. There may be some areas where these lines of intersection are discontinuous because particular polygons are spanning between three layers rather than the usual two. In such cases, it may be helpful to draw these additional lines on the polyhedron envelope so that the boundaries of each horizontal plane are clearly delineated.

There will be a horizontal plane that corresponds to each horizontal layer of spheres in the closest packed array. As the closest packed array of spheres corresponds to a grid of equilateral triangles, so will the polygon that describes the boundary of a given horizontal layer. On the cardboard surface, lay out grids of equilateral triangles with the edge equal to the sphere diameter of 1¼-inches (3.2 cm). A complex polygon for each layer of spheres will be drawn over such a grid of equilateral triangles [4.43]. Note that some layers will consist of more than one polygon corresponding to levels where the shape of polyhedron branches out in more than one direction (Level 1).

In most instances, the corners — convex or concave — of the boundary polygon will exactly fall on vertices of the equilateral triangular grid upon which the polygon is constructed. Some corners, however, do not fall on this triangular grid. When these types of corners occur, they fall without exception at points that bisect the edges of the equilateral triangular grid. The location of these corners can be determined by carefully studying the polyhedron envelope derived from the sphere packing model.

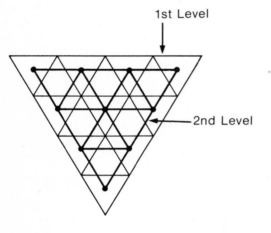

1st Level

2nd Level

4.44

When the horizontal levels are completely drawn on the cardboard surface, carefully cut them out with an X-Acto knife or mat knife. These polygonal planes must then be juxtaposed in their proper geometric relationship to one another. This can be accomplished by cutting small wood spacer blocks whose heights are equal to the space between the planes. This dimension turns out to be approximately 1 inch (2.5 cm) allowing for the thickness of the cardboard. With an appropriate number of 1-inch (2.5 cm) spacer blocks, usually two or three per level, proceed to assemble the set of polygon levels. The most difficult aspect of this phase is the correct orientation of subsequent layers. Once again, the polyhedron envelope model must be relied upon. Even with the model, some good instincts about the geometry of three-dimensional space will be required.

The most fundamental guide in establishing the vertical relationship of horizontal planes has its origins in the sphere packing layers. Remember that spheres in the second layer lie directly above the space between the spheres in a first layer [4.31]. This means that the vertices of a second grid level of equilateral triangles will lie above the exact centers of alternating triangles in a first grid level of equilateral triangles [4.44]. This principle can be directly applied to the orientation of one horizontal plane to the next, since the polygonal planes are drawn upon grids of equilateral triangles corresponding to the sphere packing layers.

With the orientation established, use push pins or thumb tacks to temporarily hold the polygonal levels to the 1-inch (2.5 cm) spacer blocks. The entire structure may be assembled in this way, or any logical combination of partial assemblies may be used if this is more manageable.

When the polygonal levels are stable and correctly spaced, proceed to add the struts to the assembly. Cut strut lengths as they are glued in place. The lengths will correspond to the edges of the six basic triangles shown in [4.38] from which the polygonal faces of the polyhedron envelope have been derived. These edge lengths may have to be adjusted here and there to allow for the thickness of both the struts and the cardboard planes.

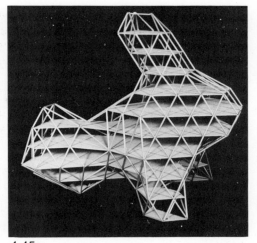

4.45a

4.45b

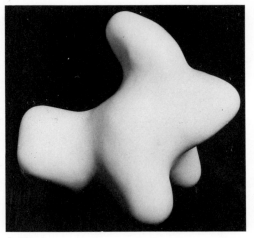

4.45c

As the planes are fixed permanently by the glued-in-place struts, the spacer blocks may be removed. Continue the process until struts are positioned at all locations given by the edges of the six basic triangles. When the glue is dry, and the structure is secure, remove all remaining spacer blocks.

At this point, the enormous strength-to-weight characteristics of such a structure will become readily apparent. Push on the structure at various points. It is extraordinarily rigid. This stems, once again, from the inherent stability provided by the fully triangulated framework. As was anticipated, local stability is provided by the horizontal planes.

In Problem 2, Chapter 3, we stated that the random assembly of cubes can be considered a metaphor representing a collection of functional, social, and aesthetic parameters embodied in a three-dimensional spatial diagram. As a three-dimensional representation of design constraints, or extrinsic forces, it governed the form response of the minimum-maximum envelope.

Although we are still operating at a high level of abstraction, the framework structure just developed suggests an architectural response to the constraints imposed by the random cube assembly, and in turn, the minimum-maximum envelope [4.45a-c]. Indeed, an efficient structure, assembled from a simple inventory of components, whose form is responsive to a complex set of three-dimensional constraints has been fabricated [4.46a-d]. It suggests that adaptive solutions to questions of architectural form can result from the interaction of extrinsic and intrinsic forces.

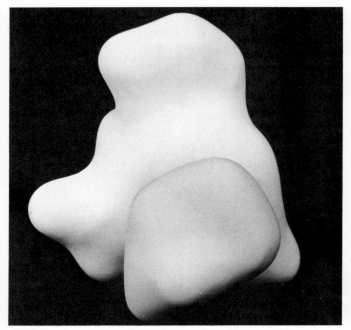

4.46a

4.46b

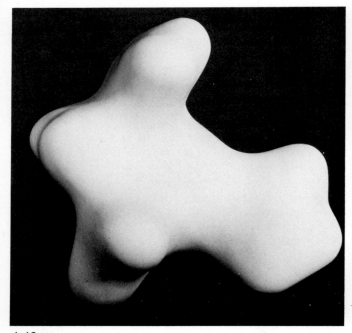

4.46c

4.46d

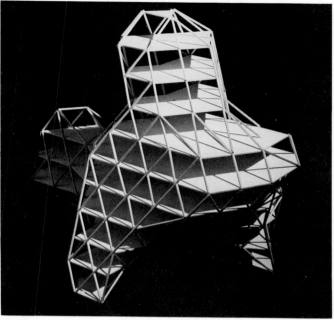

4.47a

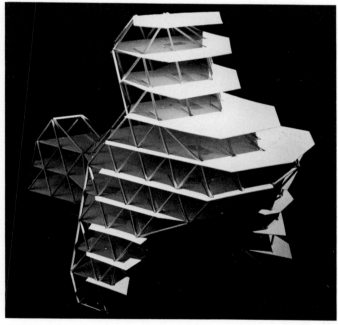

4.47b

Problem 7: Adaptation of Framework Structure Supporting Horizontal Planes to Control of Radiant Energy

Problem

Effect an adaptation of the framework structure of Problem 6 to the control of a fixed overhead light source such that the horizontal planes falling within the original envelope of the structure are entirely in the shade. This may be accomplished by a combination of orientation of the form relative to the light source and by the addition of supplementary overhanging surfaces designed to produce shade [4.47a-b]. The form should be rotated relative to the light source in order to minimize the need for additional light controlling surfaces. The overhanging surfaces for controlling light should be no larger than absolutely necessary and should occur only when absolutely necessary.

Extrinsic Forces

Location of the light source relative to the position of the structure, and overall shape of the structure.

Intrinsic Forces

Rotational orientation of the form relative to the fixed position of the light source, and the techniques with which supplementary light controlling surfaces are developed.

Conceptual Guidelines

Architectural analogies have been suggested not only in Problem 6, but in other problems as well. In such a context, there is an essential extrinsic force that has not as yet been considered. One of the primary functions of an architectural structure will increasingly have to be the control of sunlight or radiant energy. It is beyond the scope of this present foundation course to deal with this complex and interesting subject in depth. We can, however, call attention to the notion that the impact of sunlight on a structure can be controlled by design.

The primary element of solar control is the earth-sun geometry. Its product is shade. Its function is to minimize, or maximize, heat gain. Earth-sun geometry is enormously complex because of its totally dynamic character. It varies by time of day, by season, and by global location. It is a subject that is too complex for us to deal with here. (See Knowles: *Energy and Form;* and Olgyay: *Design with Climate;* and Olgyay and Olgyay: *Solar Control and Shading Devices.)* On the other hand, the subject of shade can be easily understood and manipulated.

By using a fixed light source, it is possible to learn something about the important subject of shade, while avoiding the complex subject of earth-sun geometry. In so doing, a useful and manageable introduction to the notion of controlling radiant energy can be achieved.

Techniques and Materials
Establish a fixed-point light source using a drafting or desk lamp. Its location relative to the structure is not too critical. A good position for the light source is 3 feet (914 cm) above the surface upon which the structure is resting, and 2 feet (610 cm) forward of the structure [4.48]. Fix the light source securely so that it cannot move.

When it is properly oriented with respect to the light source, slowly rotate the structure about its vertical axis. As the structure is rotated, study the pattern of light and shadows very carefully. Continue to rotate the structure until you discover the position that minimizes the amount of light falling on its internal horizontal planes. At that point, fix the position of the structure on the table.

Although by careful orientation, most of the light can be kept off the surfaces of the horizontal planes, some will inevitably find its way on to these surfaces. It is this remaining light which needs to be eliminated. This can be done by horizontally extending the surfaces of the existing planes. Such extensions will reach out beyond the boundaries of the original planes, and, of course beyond the structural framework.

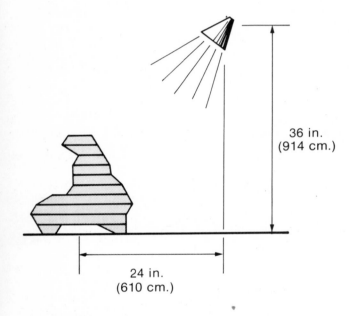

36 in.
(914 cm.)

24 in.
(610 cm.)

4.48

These horizontal extensions can be cut from white cover stock, railroad board, or 3-ply bristol board. They can overlap the existing planes to facilitate their attachment to the structure. Notches or slots will be required in order for the plane extensions to fit around the struts of the framework. It is advisable to secure the extensions by means of tape rather than cement so that adjustments can be easily made.

The shapes for the horizontal plane extensions are derived experimentally. They must be designed so that shadows are cast that exactly match the boundary shapes of the original horizontal plane surfaces. A given extension should be no larger than necessary to match shade to the level immediately below its plane of attachment. The extensions are, in effect, diagrams of the patterns in need of shade.

Remember that the goal is to provide shade within the original polygonal boundaries of the horizontal planes inside the envelope described by the framework of the structure. As extensions are added to complete the 100% shade condition within these original boundaries, the upper surfaces of the extensions will of necessity not be in the shade. Since these surfaces are external to the structural envelope, they are not required to be in the shade.

Proceed to all levels of the structure, and by trial and error, gradually eliminate all direct light within the structural envelope. When all light has been eliminated by the addition of extensions, there will be a new set of boundary conditions defined by the horizontal plane extensions.

Although these boundaries extend outside the structural envelope, they do delineate a modification to the overall form [4.49a,c,e] that is integrally related to the original envelope [4.49b,d,f]. It is a form that remains consistent with the general principles that have been explored with this series of problems. It adds further to the notion that appropriate adaptations to the forces which act upon architectural form can lead to energetically optimum design. Indeed, the natural synthesis of form is a diagram of the least energy interaction of intrinsic and extrinsic forces.

4.49a

4.49b

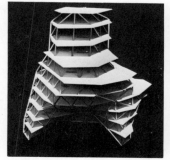
4.49c

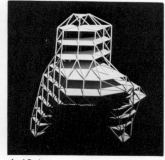
4.49d

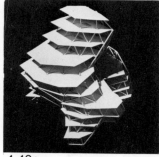
4.49e

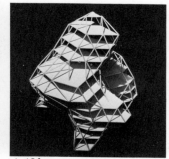
4.49f

Figure [4.50] Photographic Summary of the Integrated Problems of Chapters 3 and 4. Eight views are shown of each of eight problems of Chapters 3 and 4. Reading vertically, each model is rotated in successive 45° increments, and all models in any given horizontal row are identically oriented.

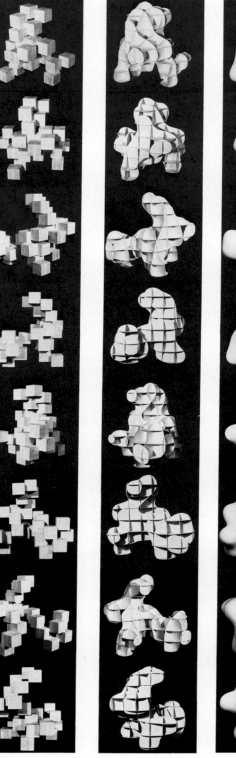
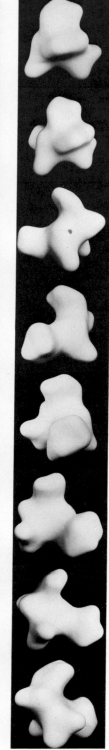

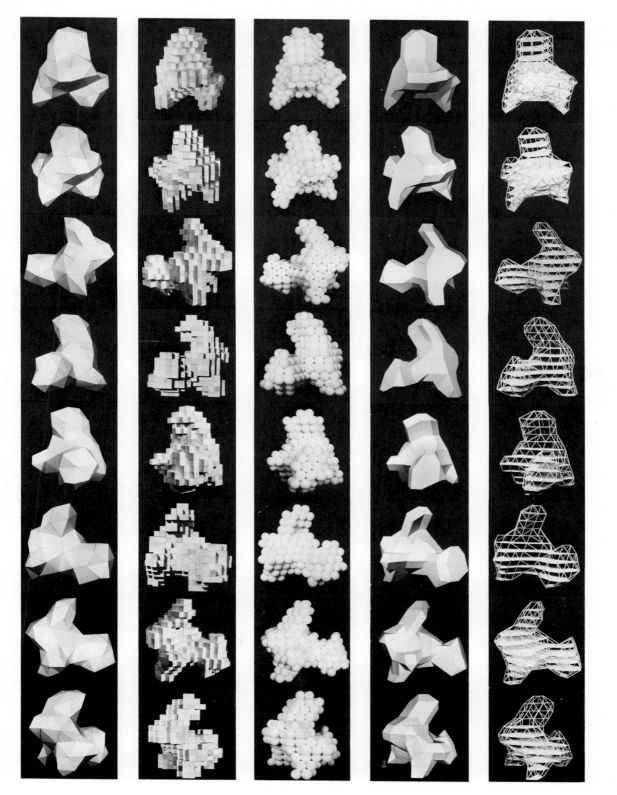

Part III
Realities of Form:
The World We Know

Chapter 5:
Form in Nature

Figure [5.1] Snowflakes. Though all are six-sided, snowflakes exhibit a great diversity of form. These form variations are the result of a least energy interaction of the intrinsic forces of its molecular structure with the extrinsic forces of environmental conditions, which include temperature, humidity, wind velocity, and atmospheric pressure. Within the limits of hexagonal symmetry, the molecular structure is an adaptive intrinsic force system that is responsive to the constantly changing environment, or extrinsic forces under which the snowflake is formed. The formative process of the snow crystal clearly demonstrates the principle that form in nature is a diagram of forces.

5.1

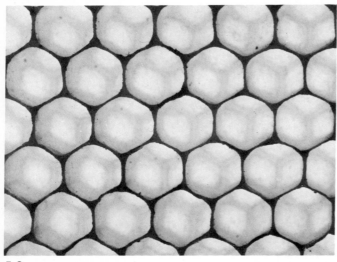

Figure [5.2] Bees' Honeycomb. The hexagonal form of a bee's honeycomb contains the greatest amount of honey with the least amount of beeswax and is the form that requires the least amount of energy for the bees to construct. The construction material, beeswax, has its own properties or intrinsic forces. The anatomical make-up and genetic instructions that enable the bees to construct a comb constitute the extrinsic force system. With astounding precision, nature coordinates intrinsic and extrinsic forces to create a structure in which economy in the use of building material is taken to its utmost limits.

5.2

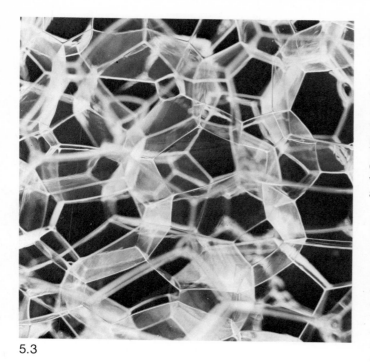

Figure [5.3] Soap Bubbles. A random array of soap bubbles is an elegant demonstration of nature's minimal principles. The forces of surface tension seek a state of stable equilibrium that satisfies the conditions of minimum potential energy. This, in turn, produces a structure in which surface area relative to volume is minimized — a multidirectional closed cell. The air pressure within each bubble presses outwardly against the membrane of soap. The froth represents the perfected minimum energy diagram of the complex array of pressure and volume differences from bubble to bubble in the array.

In all bubble arrays, all faces meet neighboring faces on common edges in sets of three at angles of 120°. All edges meet at corners in sets of four at angles of 109° 28'. When surface to volume is minimized, these angular conditions will always be met, without exception. Consistent with a condition of stable equilibrium is the observation that if a network were to connect the centers of neighboring cells in all directions, a fully triangulated three-dimensional structure would result. If such a triangulated geometry were to be constructed from rigid strut components, it would obviously give rise to a structure of enormous strength and minimum weight.

5.3

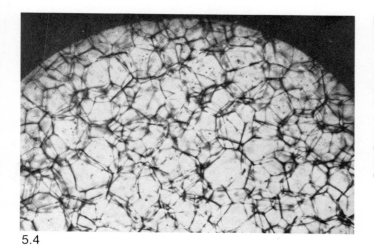

Figure [5.4] Aluminum-Tin Alloy. Following the example set by soap bubbles, this x-ray microradiograph of aluminum-tin alloy, which is magnified 15 times, reveals a structure in which the resulting form diagrams the forces of surface tension. It is no accident that its appearance is virtually identical to that of soap bubbles. When the conditions of interaction have similar properties — in this case fluid or semifluid interfaces — the overwhelming tendency toward arrangements of least energy will result in generally similar configurations.

5.4

Figure [5.5] Cracked Mud. Geometric constraints influence the patterns found in cracked mud. The natural tendency is for the simplest of all nets to be formed — one in which there are only three edges meeting at each corner. Cracking is inevitably sequential rather than simultaneous. As a result, when a crack is formed, it will typically join an existing crack by forming the ubiquitous three-rayed intersection. The formation of a four-rayed intersection is highly unlikely, though not impossible, since it is improbable that two new cracks would intersect an existing crack from opposite sides at exactly the same point. The event of cracking is, of course, the consequence of an interaction of intrinsic and extrinsic forces — the sun drying the mud or the kiln firing the glaze. Indeed, the pattern of cracks is nothing other than a diagram of this interaction of forces.

5.5

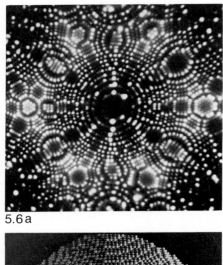

5.6a

5.6b

Figure [5.6a–b] Tungsten. The structure of tungsten metal is revealed in this field ion micrograph, magnified 600,000 times [5.6a]. Each white spot is a single atom. The atoms are organized in a very dense arrangement of great inherent stability. A model [5.6b] of hard spheres packed closely together assumes an orderly and stable arrangement that exactly corresponds to the arrangement of atoms in tungsten, and many other metals.

Principles of symmetry govern the way atoms fit together in space. These principles are given by the very nature of space itself. The specific geometry of a particular atomic arrangement results from a synthesis of the bonding characteristics of the atoms within the spatial options that are available. Intermetallic bonds tend to pull atoms together in all directions, which leads to a dense and stable geometry. As might be expected, the atomic arrangement of tungsten consists of atomic centers that are located at the nodes of a fully triangulated three-dimensional structure — a structure that is very similar to that in which soap bubbles are organized. Once again, form demonstrates arrangements in which energy is minimized.

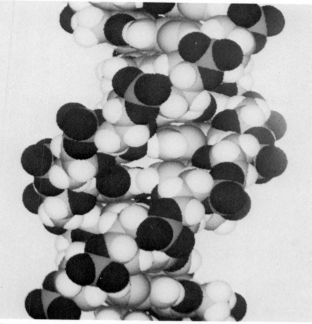

Figure [5.7] DNA Helix. The helical DNA molecule exhibits its characteristic form. We can be reasonably certain once again that this is a configuration of least effort. The particular atoms which make up the DNA molecule undoubtedly conspire to optimally arrange themselves in the double helical structure that has become so well-known. The helical form not only provides an optimum structure for the finite molecule, but anticipates and facilitates the function of replication, which is so fundamental a part of this basic structure of heredity.

5.7

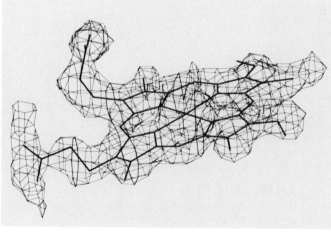

Figure [5.8] Electron Density Map. The framework defines a heme group with atomic sites at each intersection or node. The heme group is a subunit of hemoglobin, the iron-containing, oxygen-carrying molecule of the red blood cells. The contour lines represent a three-dimensional electron density map which, in effect, is the atomic environment of this biomolecule. The surface defined by the contour lines would be smooth and continuous without the sharp corners seen in this computer-generated drawing. In a sense, it is the optimal least energy package of the heme group in which surface area is minimized and stress is perfectly distributed.

5.8

Figure [5.9] Spiral Galaxy. A dramatic jump in scale from molecular events to cosmic phenomena does not alter the fundamental validity of form as a diagram of forces. Indeed, a more spectacular manifestation of form determined by forces would be difficult to imagine. Nuclear, electromagnetic, and gravitational forces are at work producing a cosmic form of astounding dimensions — the spiral form undoubtedly mapping an energetically optimum arrangement of stars and planets.

5.9

Figure [5.10] Meandering River. One of the most distinctive characteristics of rivers is their pronounced repeating pattern of curves. Meanders are not frivolous occurrences, but the form in which a river proceeds along its course with least effort. Meanders are the most probable form a river can take. They are continuous lines in which the variation in curvature is minimized, and hence are curves of minimum total work in which stress is equally and optimally distributed.

5.10

Figure [5.11] River Bank. Erosion patterns are enormously expressive of the interaction of intrinsic and extrinsic forces. The sandy bank of a salt water river, close to the Atlantic Ocean along the coast of the southeastern United States, displays constantly changing patterns of erosion. Dramatic daily cycles of the tides along with frequently choppy water and strong currents work relentlessly upon the unstable sandy shore. The sand and the organic paste that helps to bind it are vulnerable to the enormous, but simple mechanical, power of water as the receding tide is traced in the beach.

5.11

5.12

Figure [5.12] Ocean Beach. The tumultuous Atlantic Ocean pounds a corrugated pattern into the beach as it scoops sand away from the shore and deposits it out in the ocean. As the high tide begins to recede, enormous turbulence occurs under its surface. Once again, the organic paste, produced by the decaying organisms of the sea, struggles to hold the minute particles of sand together against the insatiable energy of the sea. The resulting sculptured surface diagrams the complex wave patterns resulting from this dramatic interaction of intrinsic and extrinsic forces.

5.13

Figure [5.13] Rusting Jetty. The same ocean that shapes the sandy beach does its work on an iron jetty built years ago to help stabilize the restless sand. Although the resulting form suggests an erosion pattern due to simple mechanics, it is rather a complex chemical interaction that is diagrammed by the decaying jetty. The insidious corrosive power of the salt water interacts with the intrinsic properties of iron. The result is an interactive diagram of least effort.

5.14

Figure [5.14] Bryce Canyon. The extraordinary sandstone spires of Bryce Canyon in Utah represent a long-term diagram, first of the layered build-up of the region deposited during successive stages of geological evolution, and then of gradual dissolution due to the erosive forces of water and wind. These vertically differentiated, columnar structures express the stratification of material properties. The density, hardness, and tensile strength of the layers of sandstone differ according to the variations in their chemical composition. Clearly, these relatively static variations of intrinsic properties diagram a differentiated response to the dynamic and powerful extrinsic forces that inevitably make their presence felt.

Figure [5.15] Colorado Plateau. Intrinsic and extrinsic forces have interacted to shape the great Colorado Plateau. Throughout this region, and especially in the state of Utah, are endless varieties of spectacular, large-scale examples of geologic form that diagram extraordinary force interactions. The region characteristically, although not exclusively, exhibits the warm reddish color of the ubiquitous iron oxide. The formative events that shaped the geological structure shown here were clearly very powerful. The substance of this formation, however, is much harder and less susceptible to the erosive forces that shaped the architecture of Bryce Canyon. The nuances of form remind us once again of the complexity inherent in nature's diagram of forces.

5.15

Figure [5.16] Dragonfly's Wing. A simple example in nature of a basic principle of structure is found in the wings of the dragonfly. The manner in which these pivoting wings function requires that a certain amount of stiffness be provided in the wing structure. Viewing these insect wings from an oblique angle reveals a folded structure. The deepest folds occur at the leading edges of the wings. This creates a wing structure of high stiffness relative to weight. It is also likely that aerodynamic lift is increased by the three-dimensional wing structure as it creates a virtual airfoil. High performance at low energy conspires to optimize the form of this successful creature.

5.16

Chapter 6:
Form in the Built
Environment

6.1

Figure [6.1] Mesa Verde. Mesa Verde in southwestern Colorado consists of many shallow and broad caves in which are built adobe pueblos. Built in the 12th century, the pueblos housed communities of hundreds of people. This pueblo, called Longhouse, is built in a south-facing cave and shows a particularly effective adaptation of built form to climatic forces.

The geometry of the cave, in combination with the orientation and geometry of the structures, optimizes the seasonal changes in the sun's energy. In the summer, the pueblo structures are completely in the shade during most of the day, except for early morning and late afternoon. Heat gain from the hot summer sun is thereby minimized. This photo was taken at mid-day in mid-summer. Note that the sunlight falls directly only on the mesa above the cave and on the growth in the canyon below the cave.

During the cold winter months when the sun is at a much lower angle, virtually the entire pueblo is flooded with direct sunlight for most of the day. Heat gain is, therefore, maximized. Ralph Knowles has pointed out, that although there is a natural advantage to the orientation and shape of the cave, the builders of the structures were careful to design them so that their horizontal and vertical surfaces received great benefit from the low winter sun and were protected by shade in the summer.

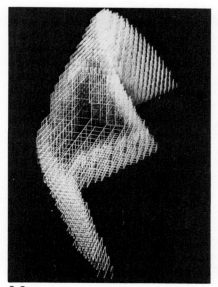

6.2a

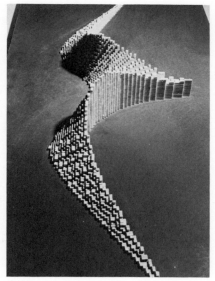

6.2b

Figure [6.2a–b] Optimum Building Forms. Ralph Knowles has proposed building forms that can be shaped and structured to minimize the effects of environmental variation through the changing seasons. These large hypothetical buildings are, in effect, diagrams of the daily and seasonal dynamics of the earth-sun geometry. Partially inspired by Mesa Verde and other pueblos in the southwest, Knowles' research has focused on the establishment of environmental equilibria through the control of daily and seasonal insulation. As in the Mesa Verde Longhouse, heat gain is minimized in the summer and maximized in the winter. Thus energy costs for cooling and heating are minimized.

A form that would literally diagram the earth-sun geometry would, of necessity, be a perfectly smooth and homogeneous shape. Since the structures shown here are intended to represent useful architectural possibilities, however, they are generated incrementally as they would be if they were constructed of real building materials. As a matter of convenience and familiarity, the building increment chosen in these examples is a cubic volume. As we have seen, this need not be the case, and in some cases the use of a non-cubic geometry could lead to further optimization. Nonetheless, Knowles has paved the way for a new approach to the generation of building design in which form can truly be considered a diagram of forces.

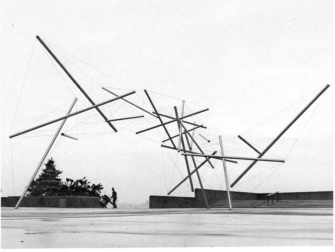

6.3

Figure [6.3] Force Diagrams in Space. Thirty years ago, the sculptor Kenneth Snelson discovered a form of structural organization in which tensile and compressive forces can be physically differentiated from one another. Since such structures, usually constructed by Snelson in stainless steel, are inherently elastic, they have little practical usefulness as load-supporting systems. Nonetheless, they do illustrate some very fundamental structural relationships and thus are valuable to contemplate.

The distribution of tensile and compressive forces through an ordinary structure is sometimes quite difficult to fully understand. Snelson's diagrams of interacting tensile and compressive forces help us to understand the nature of force distribution in structures in a fundamental way. In spite of their elasticity, they often behave like giant springs— they are stiff enough to support their own weight.

Snelson's work falls into the realm of exploration that attempts to deal in first principles. It constitutes an intrinsic force system that illuminates aspects of *a priori* governing phenomena in structural behavior. Among other things, it eloquently clarifies the necessary interdependence of tensile and compressive forces.

6.4

Figure [6.4] Reinforced Concrete Vault. This large-scale vaulted roof over an exhibition hall in Turin, Italy was designed by Pier Luigi Nervi and built in 1948. Like all of Nervi's work, its beauty derives from the elegant economy of its structural solution. The folds in the corrugated roof call to mind the folded stiffening ribs in the dragonfly's wing [5.16]. By taking advantage of the plastic qualities of reinforced concrete, Nervi deftly molds his structural form to the forces acting on the structure.

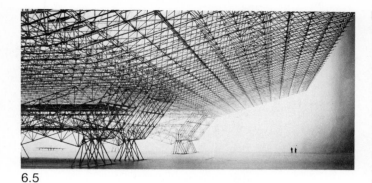

6.5

Figure [6.5] Prefabricated Space Frame. This very large, lightweight steel space frame structure was proposed by Konrad Wachsmann in the early 1950s. This, and other similar projects, called attention to the possibility of building various types of clear span structures from structural framing and connecting components that are industrially produced in standardized prefabricated units. By virtue of their highly symmetrical repeating structural patterns, such triangulated systems begin to suggest analogies to the internal arrangements of atoms in crystal, which are clearly at the heart of structural principles.

Not so surprisingly, structures of very high strength-to-weight ratios and a consequent economy of materials are typically accomplished with such systems. Recently developed sophisticated computer stress analysis techniques are the only analytical methods for demonstrating the extraordinary efficiency of such three-dimensional structures. Because of this and other factors, we have just begun to see the widespread use of space frames and related structures in architecture. Perhaps the first true space frame assembled from standardized components was built by Alexander Graham Bell in the early 1900s. We are only now just learning of their potential for creating architectural form that can truly be considered a diagram of forces.

6.6

Figure [6.6] Tensile Structures. This large-scale fabric membrane structure was designed by Frei Otto for the German Pavilion at the Montreal World's Fair, Expo '67. It is yet another approach to the problem of enclosing a large space with a lightweight, easily erected, economical structure. A grid of tension cables hanging from tall compression towers supports a fabric roof. The tension cables, are fastened to footings in the ground around the perimeter of the structure.

The tension cables responding to the force of gravity assume an arrangement of least effort. The curvatures produced by these cables are known as catenaries. The membrane defined by the grid of cables and the fabric surface itself is a surface of least area. Frei Otto pioneered such structures by studying the behavior of catenary curves and the manner in which they diagram the forces acting on them. There is probably no clearer example in the built environment of form as a diagram of forces. The diffusion of stress through the gentle compound curvatures of such a membrane tensile structure is dramatically expressed by their form.

6.7

Figure [6.7] Geodesic Dome. Developed by Buckminster Fuller, the geodesic dome is a system of structure particularly adapted to a sphere. Its geometry is derived from the Platonic Solid called the icosahedron. This figure is the most symmetrical of all possible polyhedra and can be projected onto the surface of a sphere. The spherical icosahedron can be incrementally subdivided *ad infinitum*. In so doing, it provides for the most symmetrical possible subdivisions of the sphere from which triangulated structural frameworks of various modular dimensions can be derived. Because of this most symmetrical icosahedral subdivision, the differences in the lengths of framework components are minimized.

From the standpoint of stress distribution the icosahedral subdivision results in an optimum structural framework from which to construct a sphere. Since a sphere has less surface relative to volume than any other geometric shape, this system can be quite efficient when a spherical form is particularly well suited to the objectives of a given architectural problem. The most successful applications of the geodesic dome have usually been problems requiring relatively large clear span spaces and where the large volume contained by the sphere is an advantage.

The structure shown here is a 250 ft. diameter, ¾ sphere, approximately 200 ft. high. It was the United States Pavilion at the Montreal World's Fair, Expo '67. The designers of the interior exhibition, Cambridge Seven, inventively took advantage of the large interior volume enclosed by this most elegant geodesic dome.

Figure [6.8] Radio Telescope. This 10-meter radio telescope was designed, developed, and constructed by scientists at the California Institute of Technology. Like the geodesic dome, it is another application of a space frame structure adapted to a curved surface. The space frame supports the reflector dish of the telescope. Surface accuracy and stability of the reflector dish were necessary to insure essentially perfect (diffraction-limited) reflecting surfaces for radio wavelengths as short as 1 mm or less. Fabrication techniques were developed to insure this level of accuracy in the production of the dish. The supporting structural framework, therefore, not only had to be adapted to high dimensional tolerances, but had to provide enormous stiffness and stability that is resistant to thermal stress, wind loads, and the forces of gravity.

6.8

Figure [6.9] Steel Arch Span Bridge. This bridge, completed in 1977, is the world's longest steel arch span bridge. It spans 1700 ft. over a ravine in Fayette County, West Virginia. It supports a roadway that is 3030 ft. long, and each segment of the roadway spans between 127-144 ft. The width of the bridge is 74 ft. and the longest of the vertical support columns is almost 400 ft. high. As is typical with such large vehicular bridges, the dynamic character of the loads requires that the complex array of forces acting on the structure be diagrammed with great care. This new bridge is yet another of the collection of such elegant engineering accomplishments that can be found the world over. There is no room for foolishness in bridge design.

6.9

6.10

Figure [6.10] The Crystal Palace. Designed and built by Sir Joseph Paxton in 1851 for the great architectural exhibition in London, the Crystal Palace was the first large-scale architectural project to use lightweight prefabricated modular construction. The Crystal Palace was the largest building the Victorian world had ever seen. It was possible to build the Palace in only 13 months because of the use of standardized prefabricated components of cast iron and wood whose use was repeated throughout. All components, except for the puttying for glazing, were assembled "dry" with bolts. The structure was 1848 ft. long by 456 ft. wide, and it encompassed almost one million square feet of floor area.

A little after a year from its opening, the Crystal Palace was disassembled. A newly designed Palace, using many of the components from the original building, was subsequently erected in Sydenham near London. The new building was even larger and of more complex form, although it still used the same principles of design and construction. It stood until 1936 when it was destroyed by fire.

Paxton's concept was the precursor of modern systems design in architecture. In many respects, it has yet to be equalled in its integration of sound engineering principles and the intrinsic character of modern industrial technique, even though the specific technology used by Paxton was primitive compared to what is now available 130 years later. Although it can be argued that the overall configuration of Paxton's structure was somewhat arbitrary, the form of his system demonstrated great sensitivity in the integration of intrinsic and extrinsic forces.

6.11a

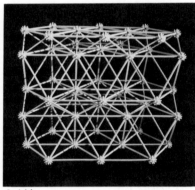

6.11b

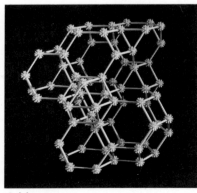

6.11c

Figure [6.11a-c] A Morphological System of Structure.
The Universal Node System was developed by Peter Pearce in order to facilitate the empirical exploration, assembly, and classification of fundamental modular network structures. Based on a study of the basic ordering principles (intrinsic force systems) of three-dimensional space, this physical model system embodies the principles of symmetry that govern arrangements of modular order. It makes such principles accessible to direct sensory experience and enables the study of modular systems, such as those that occur within the internal arrangements of atoms in a crystal, as physico-geometrical constructions rather than as analytical, algebraic abstractions.

The system consists of a Universal Node connector that has 26 spokes of differentiated cross-sections: six square, eight triangular, and twelve rectangular. Hollow branches in proportional lengths correspond in cross-sectional shape to the spokes on the node [6.11a]. The spokes are shaped in correspondence with symmetry properties given by the directions of the spokes from a common point of origin. These directions are known as symmetry axes. When networks [6.11b,c] are assembled with the Universal Node System, no matter how randomly, the shape-coded spokes insure that the nodes of the assembly always remain properly oriented with respect to one another.

This model system and its full-scale structural embodiments are manufactured and marketed by Synestructics, Inc. under the name SuperStructures®. It is the basis of a language of structural form, an intrinsic forces system, which is extensively developed in *Structure in Nature Is a Strategy for Design* by Peter Pearce. To the extent that it is derived from studies in crystallography, it can be used for depicting the internal arrangements and interconnections of atoms in crystals. Its primary focus, however, is as a morphological scheme for understanding the possible alternative arrangements and interrelationships of structure in three-dimensional space and as an actual structural system from which a wide range of human-scale structures can be designed and built with a minimum inventory of standardized components.

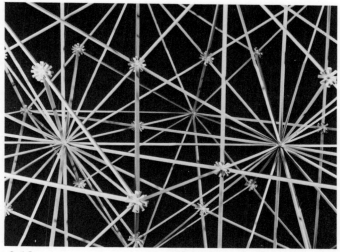

6.12

Figure [6.12] Universal Network. The Universal Node System can be used to build endless varieties of ordered and random network structures. A significant family of symmetrical, repeating networks totalling close to one hundred possibilities can be assembled with this system. This figure shows a detail of a model in which all of these possibilities, plus an infinite number of possible unsymmetrical structures, exist in one interconnected arrangement of nodes and branches—the Universal Network. Any given system can thus be considered a subset of this morphological overview.

With such a morphological strategy, it is possible to understand the relationships between seemingly unrelated structures. This kind of spatial coherence has the effect of greatly increasing the form options, and consequently the possible range of systematically structured and economically feasible design alternatives.

6.13a

6.13b

6.13c

Figure [6.13 a-c] Building as Diagram of Forces.
Using the minimum inventory/maximum diversity building system of the Universal Node, a model study was generated of a hypothetical 10-story building. The model is an attempt to show, in an impressionistic way, a probable range of form options made possible by a sophisticated intrinsic force system in response to the implied action of a range of extrinsic forces.

The rational expression of extrinsic forces in building form will most likely result in a structure that is different on all of its sides. This is because extrinsic forces do not act symmetrically upon the structure. The sun does not shine equally on all sides at all times. The wind does not act equally against all sides at all times. Gravity does not have the same effect on a tenth floor as it does on the first floor, and a building's function is not likely to be standardized from side to side and from floor to floor.

The models clearly show the possibilities for highly differentiated form using standardized components even within a single structure. The three pictures show different orientations as follows: [6.13a] west-southwest; [6.13b] south-southwest, and [6.13c] northeast. These views depict three entirely different buildings. The adaptive properties and inherent simplicity of such a sophisticated form-generating intrinsic force system facilitate the economic feasibility of building form actually generated as a diagram of forces.

6.14

Figure [6.14] Multi-Hinge Node. The economic viability of three-dimensional triangulated space structures depends on two basic parameters. Geometric configuration governs their efficiency expressed as strength-to-weight, and joining systems technology governs manufacturing and erection costs. The multidirectional geometry of the Universal Node provides possibilities for structural optimization, but in full-scale structural materials it presents a manufacturing problem of great complexity and cost. By incorporating the symmetry properties of the Universal Node into the ends of struts, which are directly connected to one another by means of simple bolted hinge components, and by carefully studying the stability characteristics of triangulated frameworks, Peter Pearce was able to design the node, as such, out of the system.

Identical simple stamped steel hinge elements are welded to the ends of round tubular steel struts in various combinations thus becoming the connectors and thereby eliminating the central hub or node. The economic advantages of this system manifest themselves relative to both original manufacturing cost and erection labor costs. This detail of structural form, far from being trivial, emerges as a diagram of intrinsic forces given by the very nature of three-dimensional space and the behavior of the framework structures within it. This multi-hinge connection system can be characterized as an optimum solution to the general problem of three-dimensional connections to the extent that it is a least common denominator.

6.15a

6.15b

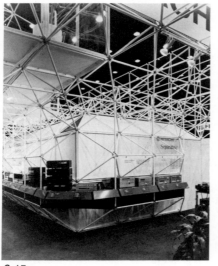

6.15c

Figure [6.15a–c] Space Frame Exhibit Structure.
Using the SuperStructures® system with its Universal Nodes, a full-scale space frame structure was designed and modeled at Synestructics, Inc. for use as a trade show product exhibit by Hitachi Corporation [6.15a]. The ground floor of this two-story structure includes stereo product displays and an enclosed theater and sound demonstration room. The second floor includes two conference rooms. An integral stairway provides access to the second floor. The structure was designed on a four-foot module and includes two lengths of strut that combine to form space frames comprised of isosceles triangles. The strut components are manufactured from 1.25 inch diameter thin-wall low-carbon steel tubing [6.15b,c].

The form of the structure evolved from criteria that came from the needs of displaying and presenting the stereo equipment and from budget constraints. The multi-hinge node [6.14] serves as the connection system—a connection system that provides for design adaptability, manufacturing ease, and great structural stability.

6.16a

6.16b

Figure [6.16a-b] Curved Space Structures. The Curved Space System is a transparent play space that incorporates a periodic continuous surface in the configuration of an 8-billion times enlargement of the environment of a diamond molecule. Children are provided with a dramatic non-Cartesian spatial experience typifying natural structure.

Designed by Peter Pearce and manufactured by Synestructics, Inc., the system consists of a pair of doubly curved, as well as flat, polygonal shell surface modules that are injection molded from transparent polycarbonate plastic. The curvatures of the surfaces are defined as an approximation of a minimal surface such as would be found in soap bubbles or thin films. When the modules are assembled by means of edge splices and vertex clamps into symmetrically repeating patterns, surface arrangements result in which membrane continuity is achieved, thereby eliminating any abrupt changes in the direction of the surface. This results in a curved structural surface that has very high strength-to-weight and in which surface area is minimized with respect to volume. These properties, once again, demonstrate least energy principles in nature, and to that extent exemplify form as a diagram of forces.

In reduction to practice, various design forces had to be taken into consideration in order to make this system work in a particular material and at a particular scale as a children's play environment. Such design forces included manufacturing constraints, materials properties, scale, safety, play value, feasibility, and economics. So even after the intrinsic force systems of a structure of this type are defined geometrically, topologically, and logistically, the extrinsic forces determined by its material, scale, and function must be reckoned with if an appropriate form is to be synthesized.

A Curved Space installation is shown in [6.16a]. The interior [6.16b] of the Curved Space structure creates a play environment that is uniquely attractive to the imagination of the child.

6.17a

Figure [6.17 a-f] Eames Chairs. In the realm of human-scale products, the principle of form as a diagram of forces is probably most clearly manifested in the furniture design of the late Charles Eames. The influence of this profoundly original work on the design profession has been of gigantic proportions. Unfortunately, for every designer who has seen the principles behind the purposeful Eamesean form, there are at least a hundred who have responded with mannerism and superficial style. One of the deceptive things about these products is their satisfying appearance. Indeed, a new aesthetic emerged from this work. The essence of the Eames approach, however, is not to be found in visual sensitivity to form and pattern, but in a sense of conceptual appropriateness rooted in a profound sense of reality.

The process by which appropriateness reveals itself in a final product is not the result of frivolous or merely egocentric aesthetic decisions. It is a complex process in which all discoverable and relevant influences are considered. Some influences, such as technical specifications and dimensions, can be easily identified and codified. Other influences, such as the optimization of form relative to both a manufacturing process and to the many ways in which a product might have to perform, remain elusive, at best. Obviously, the most difficult influences to integrate are these latter elusive ones. Usually they are the most important factors—the ones that require the intuitive leap that leads to an unpredictable solution that rings of inevitability. This integration, in Charles Eames' own words, requires a "smell of appropriateness." Few designers have mastered this sense to such an extent.

6.17b

The reduction of a chair to its most fundamental elements is manifested in the 1946 Eames molded plywood dining chair [6.17a] and low side chair [6.17b]. The molded plywood technology used by Eames demonstrated for the first time the notion of doubly curved surface elements as seat and back. These elements are supported by either a simple steel or molded plywood frame. These frames were connected by threaded inserts to simple rubber shock mounts, which were bonded to the plywood seat and back elements. This connection system, which worked very well, became an Eames trademark. The actual forms taken by the seat and back elements are so highly developed that it is difficult to imagine anything better. There is nothing arbitrary about them as they represent nearly perfect adaptation for sitting and the technological constraints under which they were produced.

6.17c

6.17d

6.17e

6.17f

Eames further explored doubly curved shell and minimal framework support structures that led; in 1950-51, to the production of two new chairs. One was a shell for a side chair that was made in one piece from molded glass-reinforced plastic [6.17c]. The other was an upholstered side chair shell made from a resistance-welded wire grid [6.17d]. Both chairs used lightweight metal support structures. One type was a four-legged tubular steel configuration, and the other was a triangulated wire space frame structure. In the case of the plastic shell, the support structure was again attached with the famous Eames rubber shock mount. The plastic side chair has now become well known, a classic in its own time—probably one of the most imitated designs ever. Produced and widely distributed by Herman Miller, Inc., it can be readily found in schools, libraries, airports, offices, and homes. Its shape is once again an optimal expression of sitting function, stress distribution, and manufacturing technology. It encompasses design principles that have forever changed the concept of a chair.

In a seemingly radical departure from earlier designs, Eames developed the Aluminum Group chair series in 1957 [6.17e,f]. These chairs were made from cast aluminum side members that support sonically-sealed upholstered tension slings. These chairs continued the Eames tradition of eliminating the superfluous. To that extent, these remarkably comfortable chairs are logical evolutionary steps from the earlier Eames concepts. The elegant simplicity and efficiency of their refined aluminum structural components work in deft collaboration with the tension membrane forming the seat/back unit.

The examples shown here represent, perhaps, the most historically significant of the Eames furniture design, if not the most influential. Many other highly successful Eames furniture systems evolved from the basic principles established with the early designs. One of the great design lessons of all time is to study deeply and thoroughly the evolution of Eames furniture design. Eamesean conceptual appropriateness reveals itself in a quality of inevitable form. The design demonstrates universal principles that transcend Eames, the man, and that become part of a design rubric. Although Eames himself never exactly described the formative process of his work as a diagram of forces, the resultant forms quite clearly suggest that Eames' sense of reality was rooted in such a concept.

6.18a

6.18b

6.18c

6.18d

6.18e

Figure [6.18a-e] Ergon Chair. The Eames furniture designs are quite clearly the antecedents of the Ergon Chair. Designed by William Stumpf and produced by Herman Miller, Inc., it is called Ergon for its deliberate attempt to optimize for ergonomic criteria. Ergonomics is the science that studies man's relationship to the physical environment. The chair is developed as a diagram of forces, and its designer collaborated with specialists in orthopedic and vascular medicine. The chair is designed not only to give orthopedically correct spinal support, but to deliberately accommodate the need to change position from time to time in order to stimulate blood circulation. It is designed to support every possible body motion while sitting including leaning forward to work at a desk, tilting back while in conversation, or stretching and relaxing. In every posture, the body is stabilized in the chair while the legs, arms, and hands are free to move.

In order to adapt the chair to the inevitable broad range of body size and shape, a range of adjustments are easily accomplished while sitting in the chair. There are no hard or sharp edges to jab the user—just soft rounded surfaces of form that provide both protection and adaptive support exactly where it is needed. Such important details are often given far less attention than they deserve.

As we have seen in the Eames chairs, the form of the Ergon chair is reduced to absolute essentials. Once again, this is not done in a simplistic visual manner, but as a response in depth to the optimization of performance expectations. The form of these Ergon chairs is subtle, incorporating nuances directed toward ergonomic, structural, and manufacturing performance. Even the form of the pedestal base is the result of such attention to performance. It seems remarkable, at first, that the seat/back shapes of the Ergon chairs suggest the early Eames plywood chairs. It must be the appropriateness of their respective forms, indeed their inevitability, as they diagram the forces to which they must be responsive.

6.19a

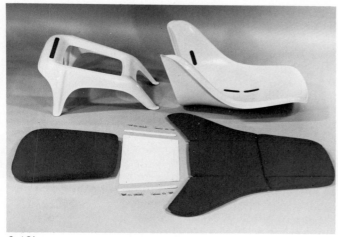

6.19b

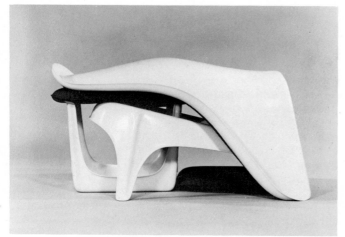

6.19c

Figure [6.19 a-f] Plastic Lounge Chair System.
Designed and prototyped in the early 1960s by Peter Pearce, this lounge chair system [6.19a] was an attempt to reduce the ratio of cost to quality by simplifying the chair structure and form to the fewest possible mass producible components [6.19b]. Part of the strategy was to also minimize production labor by designing the system for easy assembly by the consumer. Part of the consumer assembly logistics was the need for a compact shipping unit [6.19c].

The chair system is comprised of two molded reinforced plastic components—a seat/base unit and a back unit—plus a tension membrane to increase resiliency in the seat area, a seat cushion, and a one-piece segmented back cushion. These upholstered cushions were designed so that they could be sonic welded while flat, and, in the case of the back cushion, segmented along optimum hinge axes that enable the flat pad to readily adapt to the doubly curved back shell. The cushions are secured by Velcro fasteners that are bonded to the shells and sewed to the pads. The pads may be easily removed for cleaning or replacement. The hardware consists of four carriage bolts, washers, wing nuts, and a pair of longitudinal brackets, which secure the seat membrane while they clamp the two shell components of the chair together. Two sets of bolt holes, with a one-inch variation, are provided so that during assembly the user may choose the most suitable seat depth. The chair can literally be assembled by the consumer in less time than it takes to unpack it, and no tools are required.

6.19d

6.19e

6.19f

In addition to the basic seat and back shell components, the system includes two other shell moldings. One of these can function as an ottoman [6.19d] or as a small end table [6.19e]. The other molding is a second back shell which, when attached to the original seat/base molding, forms a low back lounge chair [6.19e,f].

The form of this seating system, once again, evolved out of considerations directed toward optimizing performance. The criteria for such performance stem from varied, and sometimes even totally unrelated or conflicting, influences (extrinsic forces). Strongly influenced by the Eames doubly curved shells of plywood and plastic, an early decision was made to use the shape of a resilient supporting structure itself as the main comfort-providing component. The relatively thin upholstered cushions serve to eliminate the surface hardness and physical coldness that characterize the plastic shell. Obviously, such a strategy lends itself to large simply molded components, which in addition to great unit cost advantages, have simplified assembly.

The actual forms of these molded components attempt to synthesize or diagram three basic force systems as follows. (1) Ergonomic requirements must include not only basic sitting comfort, but freedom of movement, and protection against the possibility of bumping into or falling against the chair. (2) The structural configuration of the stressed-skin doubly curved shell must provide adequate stiffness through appropriate contouring, while at the same time avoiding abrupt changes in surface direction. This will insure the maximum distribution of stress, a fundamental characteristic of shell structures. Termination of base and back shells must be accomplished in a manner that preserves structural integrity and insures stability. Particularly important is the manner in which the concentrated loads are transferred into the base shell where the base contacts the floor. (3) Manufacturing technology requires configurations which, although they may include compound curvature, they must be producible from simple molds without undercuts and with reasonable parting line conditions around their perimeters. Material flow during the molding process is also important to both cycle time and part quality. A properly designed shell structure, i.e., one that avoids stress concentrations will generally provide for good material flow.

In addition to these three basic force systems, there is a myriad of other influences. Some of these are explicit, such as ease of maintenance. Others, such as quality of finish, are implicit in the level of refinement and sophistication that follows from an attention to nuances of form—a requirement of a performance-oriented design strategy. Indeed, the design of this chair system incorporates an attitude about the determination of the form that attempts to minimize arbitrary gestures as much as possible, i.e., to fine-tune the superfluous out of the system. Even in the environment of modern furniture design, not to mention traditional furnishings, the notion that performance is the primary form determinant is not commonly held. Indeed, furniture is still, for the most part, viewed as an aspect of style or decoration, and as such becomes an important element of status. Such arbitrary form is determined by the shifting winds of the fashionable, and is not rooted in the depth, complexity, and nuance of the natural world.

Figure [6.20 a-d] Aerodynamically Ideal Automobile.
The incorporation of the philosophy of form as a diagram of forces in design methodology requires that performance objectives be dominant. We have cited examples of performance-oriented design in various examples of built form. In the area of transportation, one might anticipate that performance-oriented goals would dominate the design process. This is certainly true of naval architecture and aircraft design. Aircraft design, in fact, is perhaps the quintessential example of form as a diagram of forces. Even in the most casual observation of aircraft, one senses that arbitrary decisions about its form are reduced to an absolute minimum. Indeed, there is little room for whim and egocentric aesthetics in this field. The ability of an airplane to function at all, let alone safely and efficiently, is so completely dominated by cause and effect relationships in the physical world, that a design approach based on any other strategy has never been an option. In spite of this, or perhaps because of this, "ugly" airplanes are difficult to find.

By contrast, the design of the automobile has been dominated by excessive amounts of arbitrariness. This has been especially true in the United States for at least the past 40 years. Detroit automotive design has not been distinguished by a design response dominated by performance considerations of any sort. A fundamental element of any performance-oriented design is efficiency—a notion virtually nonexistent in U.S. automotive design. The absence of a responsible performance-oriented design approach is a curious posture for a country whose life style, city design, and resources are so totally dominated by the presence of the automobile. The automobile is at once a technically interesting consumer product, an object of utility and sport, a source of environmental stress, and a source of mechanized romanticism. It is clearly a product that could benefit from a performance-oriented approach in its design. Because of its general complexity and the necessity for it to exist in a context of physical dynamics, it can be a subject of some interest from the standpoint of form as a diagram of forces.

6.20a

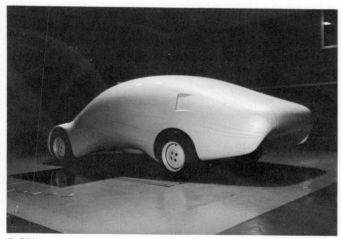

6.20b

Until recently, aerodynamic considerations in automobile design have been largely limited to applications in sports and racing cars, where high performance has always been the goal. Minimizing aerodynamic drag has been understood as an objective for many years, and in recent years other aerodynamic effects such as down force have become increasingly important. Since the recent, and belated, global awareness of the need to conserve energy has penetrated public consciousness, a mandate has emerged requiring more fuel-efficient automobiles. Designers of sports and race cars used in endurance racing have known for years that not only can acceleration and top speed be increased by careful aerodynamic design, but that substantial gains in fuel economy can be realized as well. As fuel and raw material resources become increasingly precious, optimization for performance has become as important for passenger cars as it has always been for race cars. Admittedly, the specific performance objectives may have a different emphasis, but the absolute need to direct formative processes along the lines of performance objectives is the same.

A theoretical and experimental research project on an ideal aerodynamic form for a passenger car was undertaken in 1977-78 by the Italian design firm of Pininfarina. Using computer design techniques and a sophisticated wind tunnel, an attempt was made to develop a very low-drag car the size of a standard European passenger car. Capacity for four or five adults plus a sensible-sized luggage space were included. The results of this effort were first modeled in half-scale and then ultimately in full-scale models, which were tested in the wind tunnel to demonstrate their effectiveness and calculate their drag coefficients [6.20a–d]. The lower the number of the drag coefficient, the less drag a form has. Since most production cars have drag coefficients in the range of .40 to .50, the drag coefficient of .17 in the Pininfarina model is an astounding result. When other elements of the car, such as vents, suspension, steering, and transmission are added to the model the drag coefficient is raised to .23—still an incredible result. Such a drag coefficient could produce a fuel savings over standard passenger cars of 30% or more.

6.20c

6.20d

The actual form of this proposed automobile is quite literally a diagram of forces. Not so surprisingly, its form incorporates universal principles that transcend automobile design and exemplify fundamental issues in the design of built form. The design strategy used in the Pininfarina model was aimed at achieving the maximum reduction of three different forms of drag that characterize a vehicle: form drag, induced drag, and drag due to surface friction.

Form drag is minimized by making air pressure variations as gradual as possible in order to create the smoothest possible airflow along the longitudinal axis of the vehicle. This principle is directly analogous to the principle of continuity in which variation of curvature is minimized in order to optimize the distribution of stress. The air may proceed over the form with least effort. The design response to this type of drag is to create a form which is gentle in its transitions from one surface orientation to another—almost the classic teardrop or streamlined form.

Induced drag is minimized or eliminated by reducing aerodynamic lift to zero. The overall shape and arched underside of the Pininfarina experiment accomplished this goal [6.20c]. Drag due to surface friction requires minimizing the surface area of the body form relative to the volume enclosed by the form. In combination with form drag, this is the parameter that gives the body its generally soft contour. An added bonus in minimizing surface relative to volume is that less material is required to build the body. This saves material resources and reduces the total vehicle weight, which in turn saves fuel.

The enveloping form of this proposed automobile is an optimum enclosure shell determined by the interaction of intrinsic and extrinsic forces. The intrinsic forces are comprised of the spatial needs of passenger and luggage compartments, engine, drive train, suspension, and wheels. The extrinsic forces are primarily those that result from aerodynamic considerations. A more literal example of built form as a diagram of forces is difficult to imagine.

6.21a

6.21b

Figure [6.21 a-g] Porsches. In the realm of existing consumer products, Porsche automobiles are probably one of the best examples of form as a diagram of forces. In these vehicles, arbitrariness in the form and details of the product have been absolutely minimized. Like the Eames chairs, Porsche-designed cars have been extremely influential and have survived one style trend after another, still looking as fresh today as when they were first introduced.

The predecessor of the Porsche, as we know it today, was a Porsche-designed Volkswagen sports car that was built to run in the cancelled 1938 Berlin-Rome cross country race. The form of this car [6.21a] anticipated, not only subsequent later Porsche designs, but the very interesting Pininfarina car shown above [6.20a–d]. In looking at this 1938 Porsche design, compared to the Pininfarina car of 40 years later, one can see that, of the three forms of drag, all but induced drag have been effectively considered. Specifically, form drag appears to have been minimized by a smooth and flowing shape, which envelops the spatial components of the vehicle with minimal variations in curvature. Drag due to surface friction was likely to have been minimized by the obvious reduction of surface-to-volume exhibited by this shape. Since, based upon modern knowledge of aerodynamic effects lift is not likely to have been reduced to zero, we can assume that induced drag was not minimized. Nonetheless, without computer modeling techniques and sophisticated wind tunnel experiments, the designers intuited a rather refined form responsive to the aerodynamic forces that were likely to act upon it.

In 1949 the first Porsche production car was introduced, the famous Type 356. It was produced in all of its variations for 16 years [6.21b]. Later models included slight revisions that changed the appearance very little. Like the original 1938 Volkswagen race car, the Type 356 was completely devoid of the superfluous. The form had evolved into something that was more practical as a road car and from the standpoint of manufacturing constraints. Compared to the typical automobile of the early 1950s, it was extremely radical and sophisticated. It had very low drag, and very high stiffness-to-weight due to an advanced unit frame body structure. These features resulted in remarkable performance, even though the engine had a

6.21c

6.21d

very small displacement (1600cc). Indeed, its relatively high power-to-weight ratio, low rolling resistance due to low overall weight (2000 lbs), small section tires, and low drag provided not only for impressive acceleration and high cruising speed, but also for remarkable fuel economy of about 25-30 mpg. In addition, the extremely stiff chassis, in combination with sophisticated four wheel independent suspension, provided for unprecedented handling in a road car. Once again, surface-to-volume is minimized, and the integrated continuity of doubly curved surfaces contributed greatly to smooth airflow as well as structural efficiency.

The Porsche Type 356 evolved into the now famous 911 series [6.21c]. Originally introduced in 1963, it is still one of the most sophisticated automobiles currently in production. It has undergone significant refinement during its 16 years of production, but its appearance and components have remained essentially unchanged. The performance and handling of a 911 are exemplary. The envelope incorporates the basic principles of form that were established with the 356—similar size, smooth air flow, and similar surface-to-volume ratio all resulting in a relatively low drag coefficient. Spoilers on later model 911's virtually eliminate induced drag or lift. These techniques were developed to a high degree with Porsche racing cars derived from the 911 series [6.21d].

6.21e

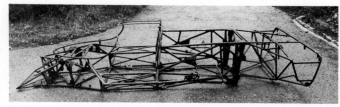

6.21f

6.21g

Like aircraft design, the design of a race car demands optimum form. Porsche's successful race car, the 917K, was an optimum compromise between minimum weight and lowest drag [6.21e]. The smooth enveloping shape was supported by a very lightweight tubular space frame structure [6.21f]. The exigencies of automobile racing create a context for design in which the forces that determine form are exaggerated. This serves to focus the design effort toward unequivocal performance objectives. Porsche's experience in racing has provided an intense laboratory for testing various design and engineering principles, which could not be duplicated artificially. These principles have not only been incorporated into Porsche passenger cars, but have contributed to the evolutionary improvement in passenger cars in general.

The most recent passenger car to emerge from the Porsche factory is the 928 [6.21g]. Like its predecessors, it is a study of pure form. Devoid of any ornamentation, its rounded smooth form bespeaks of good air flow, minimal surface-to-volume ratio, low induced drag, and efficient structure. As one reflects upon the nuances of form in Porsche automobiles, it becomes apparent that their form can be considered a diagram of forces.

6.22

Figure [6.22] Efficient Space Utilization in Automobiles.
Performance in automobile design is usually associated with a vehicle's power-to-weight ratio, which determines its rate of acceleration and, along with aerodynamic characteristics, its top speed. Recently, fuel economy has been considered an element of performance as well. The "architecture" of an automobile can also be considered in terms of performance. That is to say, how efficiently can the space enclosure system contain the passengers, their luggage, and the mechanical components of the car? How small, and presumably how light, a total package can be built that adequately encloses all of the required spatial elements.

This space utilization efficiency has probably reached its highest level of performance in the design of the Volkswagen Rabbit [6.22]. In this vehicle, a remarkably roomy cabin and generous luggage space are contained within the limits of very small overall dimensions. The configuration and form of this vehicle evolved from the performance criteria of efficient space utilization. The effectiveness of this solution was very much a function of the layout of the mechanical components.

A transverse front-mounted engine with front wheel drive via independent suspension, and an independent rear wheel suspension of novel design, left the greatest amount of room for central cabin and luggage space. The small overall dimensions with minimum overhang in the front and rear resulted in a minimum overall weight. As a consequence, a small efficient engine was able to provide a very good power-to-weight ratio, as well as further increase the efficiency of space utilization. The result is a car with respectable acceleration, comfortable cruising speed, and extraordinary gas mileage.

While the overall configuration of the Rabbit is quite reasonable and clearly efficient, it does suffer from some arbitrariness in its details. Various unnecessary creases and folds and a deliberate exaggeration of its box-like form increase surface area and betray its fundamental integrity. It is likely that its aerodynamics could have been improved through better airflow and a reduction of surface area. In spite of these criticisms, it is otherwise an important step in the evolution of a generic automotive form. It is a design of unquestionable effectiveness and calls attention to the concept of efficient space utilization as an important performance criterion.

Bibliography

Bentley, W.A., and Humphreys, W.J. *Snow Crystals.* New York: Dover, 1962.

Caplan, Ralph. *The Design of Herman Miller.* New York: Whitney Library of Design, Watson-Guptill Publications, 1976.

Drexler, Arthur. *Charles Eames-Furniture from the Design Collection.* New York: The Museum of Modern Art, 1973.

Fitch, James Marston. *American Building—The Environmental Forces that Shape It.* New York: Schocken Books, 1975.

Knowles, Ralph L. *Energy and Form. An Ecological Approach to Urban Growth.* Cambridge: The MIT Press, 1974.

Mainstone, Rowland. *Developments in Structural Form.* Cambridge: The MIT Press, 1975.

McHale, John. *R. Buckminster Fuller.* New York: Braziller, 1962.

McHarg, Ian. *Design with Nature.* Garden City: Natural History Press, 1969.

Mueller, E.W. "Atoms Visualized." *Scientific American.* June 1957, pp. 113-122.

Mueller, E.W. "Field Ion Microscopy." *Science.* 149:591-601, 1965.

Nervi, Pier Luigi. *Aesthetics and Technology in Building.* Cambridge: Harvard University Press, 1965.

Olgyay, Aladar, and Olgyay, Victor. *Solar Control and Shading Devices.* Princeton: Princeton University Press, 1957.

Olgyay, Victor. *Design with Climate. Bioclimatic Approach to Architectural Regionalism.* Princeton: Princeton University Press, 1963.

Otto, Frei. *Tensile Structures.* Cambridge: The MIT Press, 1967.

Pearce, Peter. *Structure in Nature Is a Strategy for Design.* Cambridge: The MIT Press, 1978.

Pearce, Peter, and Pearce, Susan. *Polyhedra Primer.* New York: Van Nostrand Reinhold Company, 1978.

Rudofsky, Bernard. *Architecture without Architects.* New York: The Museum of Modern Art, 1965.

Rudofsky, Bernard. *The Prodigious Builders.* New York: Harcourt Brace Jovanovich, 1977.

Smith, C.S. "The Shape of Things." *Scientific American.* January 1954, pp. 58–64.

Thompson, D'Arcy Wentworth. *On Growth and Form.* Vols. I, II. London: Cambridge University Press, 1963.

Wachsmann, Konrad. *The Turning Point of Building.* New York: Reinhold, 1961.

Photo and Picture Credits

Illustrations not listed here are by Peter Pearce and Susan Pearce.

5.4	C.S. Smith and W. Williams
5.6a-b	E. Mueller
5.7	Richard J. Feldmann
5.8	F. Scott Mathews and Edmund W. Czerwinski
5.9	Hale Observatories
5.10	U.S. Department of the Interior, Geological Survey
6.2a-b	Ralph Knowles
6.3	Kenneth Snelson
6.4	R.J. Mainstone
6.8	California Institute of Technology, R.B. Leighton
6.9	United States Steel
6.10	R.J. Mainstone
6.15b-c	Roger Conrad
6.17a-e	Herman Miller, Inc.
6.17b-d,f	Office of Charles and Ray Eames
6.18a-e	Herman Miller, Inc.
6.20a-d	Carrozzeria Pininfarina-Torino
6.21a-b, d-g	Dr.Ing.H.c.F. Porsche Aktiengesellschaft
6.22	Volkswagen of America

Index